TEXTBOOK OF ELECTROCHEMISTRY

TEXTBOOK OF ELECTROCHEMISTRY

By

Dr. Syed Aftab Iqbal

M.Sc., Ph.D., FICS

FICC, FIAEM, MNASc.

Professor

Department of Chemistry

Saifia Science College

Barkatullah University

Bhopal (India)

&

Dr. Ishaq Zaafrani

Assistant Professor

Department of Chemistry

Um-Al-Qurah University

Makkah-Al-Mukarrama

Kingdom of Saudi Arabia

DPH

DISCOVERY PUBLISHING HOUSE PVT. LTD.

NEW DELHI-110 002

Published by:
Namit Wasan
DISCOVERY PUBLISHING HOUSE PVT. LTD.
4383/4B, Ansari Road, Darya Ganj
New Delhi-110 002 (India)
Phone : +91-11-23279245; 23253475; 43596065
E-mail : discoverybooksindia@gmail.com
discoverypublishinghouse@gmail.com
namitwasan9@gmail.com
web : www.discoverypublishinggroup.com

First Edition: **2011**

ISBN: 978-81-8356-835-7

Textbook of Electrochemistry

Printed at:
Infinity Imaging Systems
Delhi

Preface

Electrochemistry is a branch of chemistry that studies chemical reactions which take place in a solution at the interface of an electron conductor (a metal or a semiconductor) and an ionic conductor (the electrolyte), and which involve electron transfer between the electrode and the electrolyte or species in solution.

If a chemical reaction is driven by an external applied voltage, as in electrolysis, or if a voltage is created by a chemical reaction as in a battery, it is an electrochemical reaction. Chemical reactions where electrons are transferred between molecules are called oxidation/reduction (redox) reactions. In general, electrochemistry deals with situations where oxidation and reduction reactions are separated in space or time, connected by an external electric circuit to understand each process.

The 16th century marked the beginning of electrical understanding. During that century the English scientist William Gilbert spent 17 years experimenting with magnetism and, to a lesser extent, electricity. For his work on magnets, Gilbert became known as the *"Father of Magnetism."* He discovered various methods for producing and strengthening magnets.

In 1663 the German physicist Otto von Guericke created the first electric generator, which produced static electricity by applying friction in the machine. The generator was made of a large sulfur ball cast inside a glass globe, mounted on a shaft. The ball was rotated by means of a crank and a static electric spark was produced when a pad was rubbed against the ball as it rotated. The globe could be removed and used as source for experiments with electricity.

In 1902, The Electrochemical Society (ECS) was founded. In 1909, Robert Andrews Millikan began a series of experiments to determine the electric charge carried by a single electron.

In 1923, Johannes Nicolaus Brønsted and Thomas Martin Lowry published essentially the same theory about how acids and bases behave, using an electrochemical basis.

Arne Tiselius developed the first sophisticated electrophoretic apparatus in 1937 and some years later he was awarded the 1948 Nobel Prize for his work in protein electrophoresis.

A year later, in 1949, the International Society of Electrochemistry (ISE) was founded.

By the 1960s–1970s quantum electrochemistry was developed by Revaz Dogonadze and his pupils.

There are various extremely important electrochemical processes in both nature and industry, like the coating of objects with metals or metal oxides through electrodeposition and the detection of alcohol in drunken drivers through the redox reaction of ethanol. The generation of chemical energy through photosynthesis is inherently an electrochemical process, as is production of metals like aluminum and titanium from their ores. Certain diabetes blood sugar meters measure the amount of glucose in the blood through its redox potential.

The nervous impulses in neurons are based on electric current generated by the movement of sodium and potassium ions into and out of cells, and certain animals like eels can generate a powerful voltage from certain cells that can disable much larger animals.

Author

Contents

1

Introduction

Electrochemistry is a branch of chemistry that studies chemical reactions which take place in a solution at the interface of an electron conductor (a metal or a semiconductor) and an ionic conductor (the electrolyte), and which involve electron transfer between the electrode and the electrolyte or species in solution.

If a chemical reaction is driven by an external applied voltage, as in electrolysis, or if a voltage is created by a chemical reaction as in a battery, it is an electrochemical reaction. Chemical reactions where electrons are transferred between molecules are called oxidation/reduction (redox) reactions. In general, electrochemistry deals with situations where oxidation and reduction reactions are separated in space or time, connected by an external electric circuit to understand each process.

The 16th century marked the beginning of electrical understanding. During that century the English scientist William Gilbert spent 17 years experimenting with magnetism and, to a lesser extent, electricity. For his work on magnets, Gilbert became known as the *"Father of Magnetism."* He discovered various methods for producing and strengthening magnets.

In 1663 the German physicist Otto von Guericke created the first electric generator, which produced static electricity by applying friction in the machine. The generator was made of a large sulfur ball cast inside a glass globe, mounted on a shaft. The ball was rotated by means of a crank and a static electric spark was produced when a pad was rubbed against the ball as it rotated. The globe could be removed and used as source for experiments with electricity.

By the mid-18th century the French chemist Charles François de Cisternay du Fay discovered two types of static electricity, and that like charges repel each other whilst unlike charges attract. Du Fay announced that electricity consisted of two fluids: *"vitreous"* (from the Latin for *"glass"*), or positive, electricity; and *"resinous,"* or negative, electricity. This was the *two-fluid theory* of electricity, which was to be opposed by Benjamin Franklin's *one-fluid theory* later in the century.

Charles-Augustin de Coulomb developed the law of electrostatic attraction in 1781 as an outgrowth of his attempt to investigate the law of electrical repulsions as stated by Joseph Priestley in England.

In the late 18th century the Italian physician and anatomist Luigi Galvani marked the birth of electrochemistry by establishing a bridge between chemical reactions and electricity on his essay *"De Viribus Electricitatis in Motu Musculari Commentarius"* (Latin for Commentary on the Effect of Electricity on Muscular Motion) in 1791 where he proposed a *"nerveo-electrical substance"* on biological life forms.

In his essay Galvani concluded that animal tissue contained a here-to-fore neglected innate, vital force, which he termed *"animal electricity,"* which activated nerves and muscles spanned by metal probes. He believed that this new force was a form of electricity in addition to the *"natural"* form produced by lightning or by the electric eel and torpedo ray as well as the *"artificial"* form produced by friction (i.e., static electricity).

Galvani's scientific colleagues generally accepted his views, but Alessandro Volta rejected the idea of an *"animal electric fluid,"* replying that the frog's legs responded to differences in metal temper, composition, and bulk. Galvani refuted this by obtaining muscular action with two pieces of the same material.

19th Century

In 1800, William Nicholson and Johann Wilhelm Ritter succeeded in decomposing water into hydrogen and oxygen by electrolysis. Soon thereafter Ritter discovered the process of electroplating. He also observed that the amount of metal deposited and the amount of oxygen produced during an electrolytic process depended on the distance between the electrodes. By 1801 Ritter observed thermoelectric currents and anticipated the discovery of thermoelectricity by Thomas Johann Seebeck.

By the 1810s William Hyde Wollaston made improvements to the *galvanic pile*. Sir Humphry Davy's work with electrolysis led to the conclusion that the production of electricity in simple electrolytic cells resulted from chemical action and that chemical combination occurred between substances of opposite charge. This work led directly to the isolation of sodium and potassium from their compounds and of the alkaline earth metals from theirs in 1808.

Hans Christian Ørsted's discovery of the magnetic effect of electrical currents in 1820 was immediately recognized as an epoch-making advance, although he left further work on electromagnetism to others. André-Marie Ampère quickly repeated Ørsted's experiment, and formulated them mathematically.

In 1821, Estonian-German physicist Thomas Johann Seebeck demonstrated the electrical potential in the juncture points of two dissimilar metals when there is a heat difference between the joints.

In 1827 the German scientist Georg Ohm expressed his law in this famous book *"Die galvanische Kette, mathematisch bearbeitet"* (The Galvanic Circuit Investigated Mathematically) in which he gave his complete theory of electricity.

In 1832 Michael Faraday's experiments led him to state his two laws of electrochemistry. In 1836 John Daniell invented a primary cell in which hydrogen was eliminated in the generation of the electricity. Daniell had solved the problem of polarization. In his laboratory he had learned that alloying the amalgamated zinc of Sturgeon with mercury would produce a better voltage.

William Grove produced the first *fuel cell* in 1839. In 1846, Wilhelm Weber developed the *electrodynamometer*. In 1866, Georges Leclanché patented a new cell which eventually became the forerunner to the world's first widely used battery, the *zinc carbon cell*.

Svante August Arrhenius published his thesis in 1884 on *Recherches sur la conductibilité galvanique des électrolytes* (Investigations on the galvanic conductivity of *electrolytes*). From his results the author concluded that electrolytes, when dissolved in water, become to varying degrees split or dissociated into electrically opposite positive and negative ions.

In 1886 Paul Héroult and Charles M. Hall developed a successful method to obtain *aluminium* by using the principles described by Michael Faraday.

In 1894 Friedrich Ostwald concluded important studies of the electrical *conductivity* and electrolytic dissociation of organic acids.

Walther Hermann Nernst developed the theory of the *electromotive force* of the voltaic cell in 1888. In 1889, he showed how the characteristics of the current produced could be used to calculate the free energy change in the chemical reaction producing the current. He constructed an equation, known as Nernst Equation, which related the voltage of a cell to its properties.

In 1898 Fritz Haber showed that definite reduction products can result from electrolytic processes if the potential at the cathode is kept constant. In 1898 he explained the reduction of nitrobenzene in stages at the cathode and this became the model for other similar reduction processes.

The 20th Century and Recent Developments

- In 1902, The Electrochemical Society (ECS) was founded.
- In 1909, Robert Andrews Millikan began a series of experiments to determine the electric charge carried by a single electron.
- In 1923, Johannes Nicolaus Brønsted and Thomas Martin Lowry published essentially the same theory about how acids and bases behave, using an electrochemical basis.
- Arne Tiselius developed the first sophisticated *electrophoretic* apparatus in 1937 and some years later he was awarded the 1948 Nobel Prize for his work in protein *electrophoresis*.
- A year later, in 1949, the International Society of Electrochemistry (ISE) was founded.
- By the 1960s-1970s *quantum electrochemistry* was developed by Revaz Dogonadze and his pupils.

PRINCIPLES

Redox Reactions

Electrochemical processes involve redox reactions where an electron is transferred to or from a molecule or ion changing its oxidation state. This reaction can occur through the application of Oxidation and reduction.

Oxidation and Reduction

The atoms, ions, or molecules involved in an electrochemical reaction are characterized by the number of electrons each has compared to its number of protons called its *oxidation state* and is denoted by a + or a -. Thus the superoxide ion, O_2^-, has an *oxidation state* of -1. An atom or ion that gives up an electron to another atom or ion has its oxidation state increase, and the recipient of the negatively charged electron has its oxidation state decrease. Oxidation and reduction always occur in a paired fashion such that one species is oxidized when another is reduced. This paired electron transfer is called a redox reaction.

For example when atomic sodium reacts with atomic chlorine, sodium donates one electron and attains an oxidation state of +1. Chlorine accepts the electron and its oxidation state is reduced to -1. The sign of the oxidation state (positive/negative) actually corresponds to the value of each ion's electronic charge. The attraction of the differently charged sodium and chlorine ions is the reason they then form an ionic bond.

The loss of electrons from an atom or molecule is called oxidation, and the gain of electrons is reduction. This can be easily remembered through the use of mnemonic devices. Two of the most popular are *"OIL RIG"* (Oxidation Is Loss, Reduction Is Gain) and *"LEO"* the lion says *"GER"* (Lose Electrons: Oxidization, Gain Electrons: Reduction). For cases where electrons are shared (covalent bonds) between atoms with large differences in electronegativity, the electron is assigned to the atom with the largest electronegativity in determining the oxidation state.

The atom or molecule which loses electrons is known as the *reducing agent*, or *reductant*, and the substance which accepts the electrons is called the *oxidizing agent*, or *oxidant*. The oxidizing agent is always being reduced in a reaction; the reducing agent is always being oxidized. Oxygen is a common oxidizing agent, but not the only one. Despite the name, an oxidation reaction does not necessarily need to involve oxygen. In fact, a fire can be fed by an oxidant other than oxygen; fluorine fires are often unquenchable, as fluorine is an even stronger oxidant (it has a higher electronegativity) than oxygen.

For reactions involving oxygen, the gain of oxygen implies the oxidation of the atom or molecule to which the oxygen is added (and the oxygen is reduced). For example, in the oxidation of octane by oxygen to form carbon dioxide and water, both the carbon in the octane and the oxygen begin with an oxidation state of 0. In forming CO_2 the carbon loses four electrons to become C^{4+} and the oxygens each gain two electrons to be O_2^-. In organic compounds, such as butane or ethanol, the loss of hydrogen implies oxidation of the molecule from which it is lost (and the hydrogen is reduced). This follows because the hydrogen donates its electron in covalent bonds with non-metals but it takes the electron along when it is lost. Conversely, loss of oxygen or gain of hydrogen implies reduction.

Balancing Redox Reactions

Electrochemical reactions in water are better understood by balancing redox reactions using the Ion-Electron Method where H^+, OH^- ion, H_2O and electrons (to compensate the oxidation changes) are added to cell's half reactions for oxidation and reduction.

Acid Medium

In acid medium H+ ions and water are added to half reactions to balance the overall reaction. For example, when manganese reacts with sodium bismuthate.

Mn^{2+} (*aq*) + $NaBiO_3$(*s*) $\rightarrow$ Bi^{3+} (*aq*) + MnO_4^- (*aq*) $4H_2O$(*l*) + Mn^{2+} (*aq*) $\rightarrow$ MnO_4^- (*aq*) + $8H^+$ (*aq*) + $5e^-$ $2e^-$ + $6H^+$ (*aq*) + BiO_3^- (*s*) $\rightarrow$ Bi^{3+} (*aq*) + $3H_2O$ (*l*)

Finally the reaction is balanced by multiplying the number of electrons from the reduction half reaction to oxidation half reaction and vice versa and adding both half reactions, thus solving the equation.

$8H_2O(l) + 2Mn^{2+} (aq) \rightarrow 2MnO_4^- (aq) + 16H^+ (aq) + 10e^-$
$10e^- + 30H^+ (aq) + 5BiO_3^-(s) \rightarrow 5Bi^{3+} (aq) + 15H_2O(l)$

Reaction Balanced

$14H^+ (aq) + 2Mn^{2+} (aq) + 5NaBiO_3(s) \rightarrow 7H_2O(l) + 2MnO_4^- (aq) + 5Bi^{3+} (aq) + 5Na^+ (aq)$

Basic Medium

In basic medium OH^- ions and water are added to half reactions to balance the overall reaction. For example on reaction between Potassium permanganate and Sodium sulfite.

$KMnO_4 + Na_2SO_3 + H_2O \rightarrow MnO_2 + Na_2SO_4 + KOH$

$3_e^- + 2H_2O + MnO_4^- \rightarrow MnO_2 + 4OH^-$

$2OH^- + SO_3^{2-} \rightarrow SO_4^{2-} + H_2O + 2e^-$

The same procedure as followed on acid medium by multiplying electrons to opposite half reactions solve the equation thus balancing the overall reaction.

$$6e^- + 4H_2O + 2MnO_4^- \rightarrow 2MnO_2 + 8OH^-$$

$$6OH^- + 3SO_3^{2-} \rightarrow 3SO_4^{2-} + 3H_2O + 6e^-$$

Equation balanced:

$2KMnO_4 + 3Na_2SO_3 + H_2O \rightarrow 2MnO_2 + 3Na_2SO_4 + 2KOH$

Neutral Medium

The same procedure as used on acid medium is applied, for example on balancing using electron ion method to complete combustion of propane.

Reaction unbalanced: $C_3H_8 + O_2 \rightarrow CO_2 + H_2O$

Reduction: $4H^+ + O2 + 4e- \rightarrow 2H2O$

Oxidation: $6H_2O + C_3H_8 \rightarrow 3CO_2 + 20e^- + 20H^+$

As in acid and basic medium, electrons which were used to compensate oxidation changes are multiplied to opposite half reactions, thus solving the equation.

$20H^+ + 5O_2 + 20e^- \rightarrow 10H_2O$

$6H_2O + C_3H_8 \rightarrow 3CO_2 + 20e^- + 20H^+$

Equation balanced:

$C_3H_8 + 5O_2 \rightarrow 3CO_2 + 4H_2O$

Electrochemical Cells

An electrochemical cell is a device that produces an electric current from energy released by a spontaneous redox reaction. This kind of cell includes the Galvanic cell or Voltaic cell, named after Luigi Galvani and Alessandro Volta, both scientists who conducted several experiments on chemical reactions and electric current during the late 18th century.

Electrochemical cells have two conductive electrodes (the anode and the cathode). The anode is defined as the electrode where oxidation occurs and the cathode is the electrode where the reduction takes place. Electrodes can be made from any sufficiently conductive materials, such as metals, semiconductors, graphite, and even conductive polymers. In between these electrodes is the electrolyte, which contains ions that can freely move.

The Galvanic cell uses two different metal electrodes, each in an electrolyte where the positively charged ions are the oxidized form of the electrode metal. One electrode will undergo oxidation (the anode) and the other will undergo reduction (the cathode). The metal of the anode will oxidize, going from an oxidation state of 0 (in the solid form) to a positive oxidation state and become an ion. At the cathode, the metal ion in solution will accept one or more electrons from the cathode and the ion's oxidation state is reduced to 0. This forms a solid metal that electrodeposits on the cathode. The two electrodes must be electrically connected to each other, allowing for a flow of electrons that leave the metal of the anode and flow through this connection to the ions at the surface of the cathode. This flow of electrons is an electrical current that can be used to do work, such as turn a motor or power a light.

A Galvanic cell whose electrodes are zinc and copper submerged in zinc sulfate and copper sulfate, respectively, is known as a Daniell cell.

Half reactions for a Daniell cell are these:

Zinc electrode (anode) : $Zn(s)$ * Zn^{2+} (aq) + $2e^-$

Copper electrode (cathode) : Cu^{2+} (aq) + $2e^- \rightarrow Cu(s)$

In this example, the anode is zinc metal which oxidizes (loses electrons) to form zinc ions in solution, and copper ions accept electrons from the copper metal electrode and the ions deposit at the copper cathode as an electrodeposit. This cell forms a simple battery as it will spontaneously generate a flow of electrical current from the anode to the cathode through the external connection. This reaction can be driven in reverse by applying a voltage, resulting in the deposition of zinc metal at the anode and formation of copper ions at the cathode.

To provide a complete electric circuit, there must also be an ionic conduction path between the anode and cathode electrolytes in addition to the electron conduction path. The simplest ionic conduction path is to provide a liquid junction. To avoid mixing between the two electrolytes, the liquid junction can be provided through a porous plug that allows ion flow while reducing electrolyte mixing. To further minimize mixing of the electrolytes, a salt bridge can be used which consists of an electrolyte saturated gel in an inverted U-tube. As the negatively charged electrons flow in one direction around this circuit, the positively charged metal ions flow in the opposite direction in the electrolyte.

A voltmeter is capable of measuring the change of electrical potential between the anode and the cathode.

Electrochemical cell voltage is also referred to as electromotive force or emf.

A cell diagram can be used to trace the path of the electrons in the electrochemical cell. For example, here is a cell diagram of a Daniell cell:

ZN(s) Zn^{2+} (*1M*) Cu^{2+} (1M) Cu(*s*)

First, the reduced form of the metal to be oxidized at the anode (Zn) is written. This is separated from its oxidized form by a vertical line, which represents the limit between the phases (oxidation changes). The double vertical lines represent the saline bridge on the cell. Finally, the oxidized form of the metal to be reduced at the cathode, is written, separated from its reduced form by the vertical line. The electrolyte concentration is given as it is an important variable in determining the cell potential.

Standard Electrode Potential

To allow prediction of the cell potential, tabulations of standard electrode potential are available. Such tabulations are referenced to the standard hydrogen electrode (SHE). The standard hydrogen electrode undergoes the reaction.

$2H^+ (aq) + 2e^- \rightarrow H_2$

which is shown as reduction but, in fact, the SHE can act as either the anode or the cathode, depending on the relative oxidation/reduction potential of the other electrode/electrolyte combination. The term standard in SHE requires a supply of hydrogen gas bubbled through the electrolyte at a pressure of 1 atm and an acidic electrolyte with H+ activity equal to 1 (usually assumed to be $[H^+] = 1$ mol/litre.

The SHE electrode can be connected to any other electrode by a salt bridge to form a cell. If the second electrode is also at standard conditions, then the measured cell potential is called the standard electrode potential for the electrode. The standard electrode potential for the SHE is zero, by definition. The polarity of the standard electrode potential provides information about the relative reduction potential of the electrode compared to the SHE. If the electrode has a positive potential with respect to the SHE, then that means it is a strongly reducing electrode which forces the SHE to be the anode (an example is Cu in aqueous $CuSO_4$ with a standard electrode potential of 0.337 V). Conversely, if the measured potential is negative, the electrode is more oxidizing than the SHE (such as Zn in $ZnSO_4$ where the standard electrode potential is -0.763 V).

Standard electrode potentials are usually tabulated as reduction potentials. However, the reactions are reversible and the role of a particular electrode in a cell depends on the relative oxidation/reduction potential of both electrodes. The oxidation potential for a particular electrode is just the negative of the reduction potential. A standard cell potential can be determined by looking up the standard electrode potentials for both electrodes (sometimes called half cell potentials). The one that is smaller will be the anode and will undergo oxidation. The cell potential is then calculated as the sum of the reduction potential for the cathode and the oxidation potential for the anode.

$$E^0_{cell} = E^0_{red}(cathode) - E^0_{red}(anode)$$

$$= E^0_{red}(cathode) + E^0_{oxi}(anode)$$

For example, the standard electrode potential for a copper electrode is:

Cell Diagram

Pt(s) H_2 (1*atm*) H^+ (1*M*) Cu^{2+} (1*M*) Cu(*s*)

$$E^0_{cell} = E^0_{red}(cathode) - E^0_{red}(anode)$$

At standard temperature, pressure and concentration conditions, the cell's emf (measured by a multimeter) is

0.34 V. by definition, the electrode potential for the SHE is zero. Thus, the Cu is the cathode and the SHE is the anode giving

$$E_{cell} = E^0Cu^{2+}/Cu - E^0H^+/H_2$$

or

$$E^0Cu^{2+}/Cu = 0.34 \text{ V}$$

Changes in the stoichiometric coefficients of a balanced cell equation will not change E^0_{red} value because the standard electrode potential is an intensive property.

Spontaneous Process of Rodex Reaction

During operation of electrochemical cells, chemical energy is transformed into electrical energy and is expressed mathematically as the product of the cell's emf and the electrical charge transferred through the external circuit.

$$\text{Electrical energy} = E_{cell}\ C_{trans}$$

where E_{cell} is the cell potential measured in volts (V) and C_{trans} is the cell current integrated over time and measured in coulumbs (C). C_{trans} can also be determined by multiplying the total number of electrons transferred (measured in moles) times Faraday's constant(F).

The emf of the cell at zero current is the maximum possible emf. It is used to calculate the maximum possible electrical energy that could be obtained from a chemical reaction. This energy is referred to as electrical work and is expressed by the following equation:

$$W_{max} = W_{electrical} = -nFE_{cell}$$

where work is defined as positive into the system.

Since the free energy is the maximum amount of work that can be extracted from a system, one can write:

$$\Delta G = -nFE_{cell}$$

A positive cell potential gives a negative change in Gibbs free energy. This is consistent with the cell production of an electric current flowing from the cathode to the anode through the external circuit. If the current is driven in the opposite direction by imposing an external potential, then work is done on the cell to drive electrolysis.

A spontaneous electrochemical reaction (change in Gibbs free energy less than zero) can be used to generate an electric current, in electrochemical cells. This is the basis of all batteries and fuel cells. For example, gaseous oxygen (O_2) and hydrogen (H_2) can be combined in a fuel cell to form water and energy, typically a combination of heat and electrical energy.

Conversely, non-spontaneous electrochemical reactions can be driven forward by the application of a current at sufficient voltage. The electrolysis of water into gaseous oxygen and hydrogen is a typical example.

The relation between the equilibrium constant, K, and the Gibbs free energy for an electrochemical cell is expressed as follows:

$$\Delta G^0 = -\mathrm{RT} \ln K = -\mathrm{nFE}^0_{cell}$$

Rearranging to express the relation between standard potential and equilibrium constant yields

$$\mathrm{E}^0_{cell} = \frac{\mathrm{RT}}{\mathrm{nF}} \ln \mathrm{K}$$

Previous equation can use Briggsian logarithm as shown below:

$$\mathrm{E}^0_{cell} = \frac{0.0592\mathrm{V}}{\mathrm{n}} \log \mathrm{K}$$

Lithium Battery

Instead of an aqueous electrolyte or a moist electrolyte paste, a solid state battery operates using a solid electrolyte. Lithium polymer batteries are an example of this; a graphite bar acts as the anode, a bar of lithium cobaltate acts as the cathode, and a polymer, swollen with a lithium salt, allows the passage of ions and serves as the electrolyte. In this cell, the carbon in the anode can reversibly form a lithium-carbon alloy. Upon discharging, lithium ions spontaneously leave the lithium cobaltate cathode and travel through the polymer and into the carbon anode forming the alloy. This flow of positive lithium ions is the electrical current that the battery provides. By charging the cell, the lithium dealloys and travels back into the cathode. The advantage of this kind of battery is that Lithium possess the highest negative value of standard reduction potential. It is also a light metal and therefore less mass is required to generate 1 mole of electrons. Lithium ion battery technologies are widely used in portable electronic devices because they have high energy storage density and are rechargeable. These technologies show promise for future automotive applications, with new materials such as iron phosphates and lithium vanadates.

Flow Battery

Most batteries have all of the electrolyte and electrodes within a single housing. A flow battery is unusual in that the majority of the electrolyte, including dissolved reactive species, is stored in separate tanks. The electrolytes are pumped through a reactor, which houses the electrodes, when the battery is charged or discharged.

These types of batteries are typically used for large-scale energy storage (kWh - multi MWh). Of the several different types that have been developed, some are of current commercial interest, including the vanadium redox battery and zinc bromine battery.

Fuel Cell

Fossil fuels are used in power plants to supply electrical needs, however their conversion into electricity is an inefficient process. The most efficient electrical power plant may only convert about 40% of the original chemical energy into electricity when burned or processed.

To enhance electrical production, scientists have developed fuel cells where combustion is replaced by electrochemical methods, similar to a battery but requiring continuous replenishment of the reactants consumed.

The most popular is the oxygen-hydrogen fuel cell, where two inert electrodes (porous electrodes of nickel and nickel oxide) are placed in an electrolytic solution such as hot caustic potash, in both compartments (anode and cathode) gaseous hydrogen and oxygen are bubbled into solution.

The overall reaction is identical to hydrogen combustion. Oxidation and reduction take place in the anode and cathode separately. This is similar to the electrode used in the cell for measuring standard reduction potential which has a double function acting as electrical conductors providing a surface required to decomposition of the molecules into atoms before electron transferring, thus named electrocatalysts. Platinum, nickel, and rhodium are good electrocatalysts.

Corrosion

Corrosion is the term applied to metal rust caused by an electrochemical process. Most people are likely familiar with the corrosion of iron, in the form of reddish rust. Other examples include the black tarnish on silver, and red or green corrosion that may appear on copper and its alloys, such as brass. The cost of replacing metals lost to corrosion is in the multi-billions of dollars per year.

Corrosion of Common Metals

Coinage metals, such as copper and silver, slowly corrode through use. A *patina* of green-blue *copper carbonate* forms on the surface of copper with exposure to the water and carbon dioxide in the air. Silver coins or cutlery that are exposed to high sulfur foods such as eggs or the low levels of sulfur species in the air develop a layer of black *Silver sulfide*.

Gold and *platinum* are extremely difficult to oxidize under normal circumstances, and require exposure to a powerful chemical oxidizing agent such as *aqua regia*.

Some common metals oxidize extremely rapidly in air. *Titanium* and *aluminium* oxidize instantaneouly in contact with the oxygen in the air. These metals form an extremely thin layer of oxidized metal on the surface. This thin layer of oxide protects the underlying layers of the metal from the air preventing the entire metal from oxidizing. These metals are used in applications where corrosion resistance is important. *Iron*, in contrast, has an oxide that forms in air and water, called rust, that does not stop the further oxidation of the iron. Thus iron left exposed to air and water will continue to rust until all of the iron is oxidized.

Prevention of Corrosion

Attempts to save a metal from becoming anodic are of two general types. Anodic regions dissolve and destroy the structural integrity of the metal.

While it is almost impossible to prevent anode/cathode formation, if a non-conducting material covers the metal, contact with the electrolyte is not possible and corrosion will not occur.

Coating

Metals are coated on its surface with paint or some other non-conducting coating. This prevents the electrolyte from reaching the metal surface if the coating is complete.

Scratches exposing the metal will corrode with the region under the paint, adjacent to the scratch, to be anodic.

However, if the tin coating is scratched the iron becomes anodic and corrodes rapidly.

Sacrificial Anodes

A method commonly used to protect a structural metal is to attach a metal which is more anodic than the metal to be protecred corrosion. It is called "sacrificial" because the anode dissolves and has to be replaced periodically.

Other metals, such as magnesium, would work very well but zinc is the least expensive useful metal.

Thode and is protected from being oxidized and rusting. The magnesium anode is sacrificed. At intervals new ingots are buried to replace those lost.

Applications

There are various extremely important electrochemical processes in both nature and industry, like the coating of objects with metals or metal oxides through electrodeposition and the detection of alcohol in drunken drivers through the redox reaction of ethanol. The generation of chemical energy through photosynthesis is inherently an electrochemical process, as is production of metals like aluminum and titanium from their ores. Certain diabetes blood sugar meters measure the amount of glucose in the blood through its redox potential.

The nervous impulses in neurons are based on electric current generated by the movement of sodium and potassium ions into and out of cells, and certain animals like eels can generate a powerful voltage from certain cells that can disable much larger animals.

2

Chemistry and Electricity

The connection between chemistry and electricity is a very old one, going back to Alessandro Volta's discovery, in 1793, that electricity could be produced by placing two dissimilar metals on opposite sides of a moistened paper. In 1800, Nicholson and Carlisle, using Volta's primitive battery as a source, showed that an electric current could decompose water into oxygen and hydrogen. This was surely one of the most significant experiments in the history of chemistry, for it implied that the atoms of hydrogen and oxygen were associated with positive and negative electric charges, which must be the source of the bonding forces between them. By 1812, the Swedish chemist Berzelius could propose that all atoms are electrified, hydrogen and the metals being positive, the nonmetals negative. In electrolysis, the applied voltage was thought to overpower the attraction between these opposite charges, pulling the electrified atoms apart in the form of *ions* (named by Berzelius from the Greek for "travelers").

It would be almost exactly a hundred years later before the shared electron pair theory of G.N. Lewis could offer a significant improvement over this view of chemical bonding.

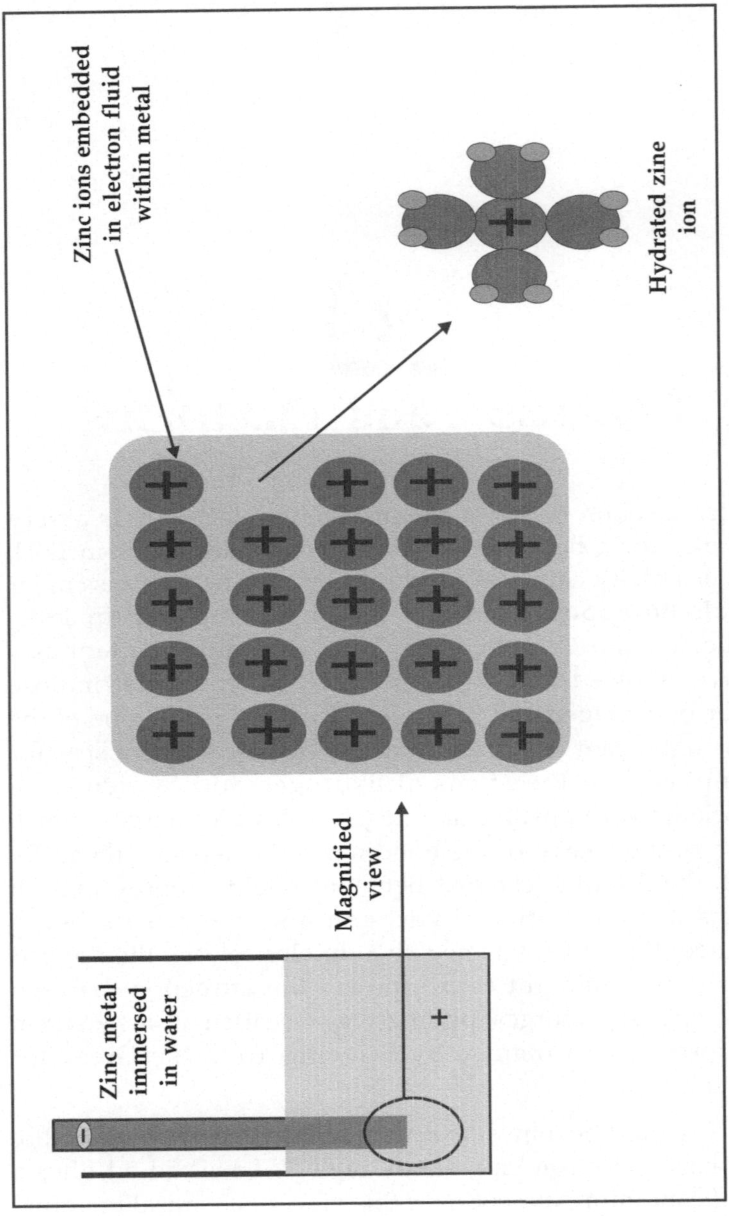

Fig. 2.1: Oxidation of metallic zinc in contact with water

Meanwhile the use of electricity as a means of bringing about chemical change continued to play a central role in the development of chemistry. Humphrey Davey prepared the first elemental sodium by electrolysis of a sodium hydroxide melt. It was left to Davey's former assistant, Michael Faraday, to show that there is a direct relation between the amount of electric charge passed through the solution and the quantity of electrolysis products. James Clerk Maxwell immediately saw this as evidence for the "molecule of electricity", but the world would not be receptive to the concept of the electron until the end of the century.

Electroneutrality

Nature seems to strongly discourage any process that would lead to an excess of positive or negative charge in matter. Suppose, for example, that we immerse a piece of zinc metal in pure water. A small number of zinc atoms go into solution as Zn ions, leaving their electrons behind in the metal:

$$Zn(s) \rightarrow Zn^{2+} + 2e^-$$

As this process goes on, the electrons which remain in the zinc cause a negative charge to build up within the metal which makes it increasingly difficult for additional positive ions to leave the metallic phase. A similar buildup of positive charge in the liquid phase adds to this inhibition. Very soon, therefore, the process comes to a halt, resulting in a solution in which the concentration of Zn^{2+} is still too low (around 10^{-10} *M*) to be detected by ordinary chemical means.

There would be no build-up of opposing charges in the two phases if the excess electrons could be removed from the metal or the positive ions consumed as the reaction proceeds. For example, we could drain off the electrons left behind in the zinc through an external circuit that forms part of a complete electrochemical cell; this we will describe later. Another way to remove electrons is to bring a good electron acceptor (that is, an *oxidizing agent*) into contact with the electrode. A suitable electron acceptor would be hydrogen ions; this is why acids attack many metals. For the very active metals such as sodium, water itself is a sufficiently good electron acceptor. The degree of charge unbalance that is allowed produces differences in electric potential of no more than a few volts, and corresponds to unbalances in the concentrations of oppositely charged particles that are not chemically significant. There is nothing mysterious about this prohibition, known as the *electroneutrality principle;* it is a simple consequence of the thermodynamic work required to separate opposite charges, or to bring like charges into closer contact. The additional work raises the free energy of the process, making it less spontaneous.

The only way we can get the oxidation of the metal to continue is to couple it with some other process that restores electroneutrality to the two phases. A simple way to accomplish this would be to immerse the zinc in a solution of copper sulfate instead of pure water. As you will recall if you have seen this commonly-performed experiment carried out, the zinc metal quickly becomes covered with a black coating of finely-divided metallic copper. The reaction is a simple oxidation-reduction process, a transfer of two electrons from the zinc to the copper:

$$Zn(s) \rightarrow Zn^{2+} + 2e^- \quad Cu^{2+} + 2e^- \rightarrow Cu(s)$$

The dissolution of the zinc is no longer inhibited by a buildup of negative charge in the metal, because the excess electrons are removed from the zinc by copper ions that come into contact with it. At the same time, the solution remains electrically neutral, since for each Zn ion introduced to the solution, one Cu ion is removed. The net reaction

$$Zn(s) + Cu^{2+} \rightarrow Zn^{2+} + Cu(s)$$

quickly goes to completion.

Potential Differences at Interfaces

The transition region between two phases consists of a region of charge unbalance known as the *electric double layer.* As its name implies, this consists of an inner monomolecular layer of adsorbed water molecules and ions, and an outer diffuse region that compensates for any local charge unbalance that gradually merges into the completely random arrange-ment of the bulk solution. In the case of a metal immersed in pure water, the electron fluid within the metal causes the polar water molecules to adsorb to the surface and orient themselves so as to create two thin planes of positive and negative charge. If the water contains dissolved ions, some of the larger (and more polarizable) anions will loosely bond (*chemisorb*) to the metal, creating a negative inner layer which is compensated by an excess of cations in the outer layer.

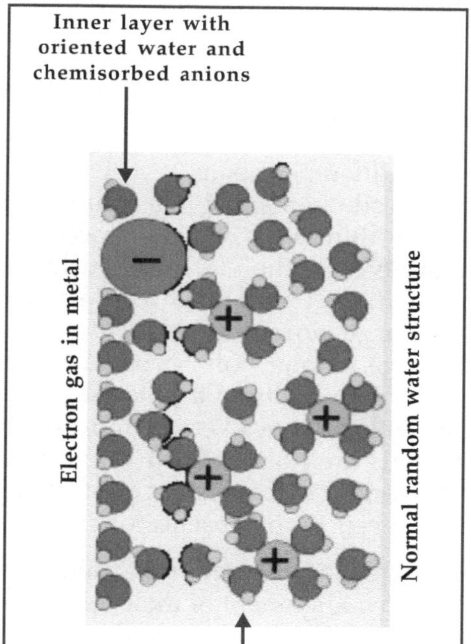

***Fig 2.2*: Electric double layer at an electrode surface**

Electrochemistry is the study of reactions in which charged articles (ions or electrons) cross the interface between two phases of matter, typically a metallic phase (the electrode) and a conductive solution, or *electrolyte*. A process of this kind can always be represented as a chemical reaction and is known generally as an *electrode process*. Electrode processes take place within the double layer and produce a slight unbalance in the electric charges of the electrode and the solution. Much of the importance of electrochemistry lies in the ways that these potential differences can be related to the thermodynamics and kinetics of electrode reactions. *In particular, manipulation of the interfacial potential difference affords an important way of exerting external control on an electrode reaction.*

The interfacial potential differences which develop in electrode-solution systems are limited to only a few volts at most. This may not seem like very much until you consider that this potential difference spans a very small distance. In the case of an electrode immersed in a solution, this distance corresponds to the thin layer of water molecules and ions that attach themselves to the electrode surface— normally only a few atomic diameters. Thus a very small voltage can produce a very large potential *gradient*. For example, a potential difference of one volt across a typical 10-8 cm interfacial boundary amounts to a potential gradient of 100 million volts per centimeter— a very significant value indeed! Interfacial potentials are not confined to metallic electrodes immersed in solutions; they can in fact exist between any two phases in contact, even in the absence of chemical reactions.

In many forms of matter, they are the result of adsorption or ordered alignment of molecules caused by non-uniform forces in the interfacial region. Thus colloidal particles in aqueous suspensions selectively adsorb a given kind of ion, positive for some colloids, and negative for others. The resulting net electric charge prevents the particles from coming together and coalescing, which they would otherwise tend to do under the influence of ordinary van der Waals attractions.

Interfacial potential differences are not directly observable

The usual way of measuring a potential difference between two points is to bring the two leads of a voltmeter into contact with them. It's simple enough to touch one lead of the meter to a metallic electrode, but there is no way you can connect the other lead to the solution side of the interfacial region without introducing a second second electrode with its own interfacial potential, so you would be measuring the sum of *two* potential differences.

3

Electrochemical Cells

Although it is physically impossible to measure or manipulate the potential difference between a piece of metal and the solution in which it is immersed, we can easily measure a potential difference between two such electrodes immersed in a solution. The result will be the sum of the two electrode potentials, we shall see farther on that such measurements can be supply all the information we need in order to characterize the two electrode reactions.

This arrangement is called a galvanic cell. A typical cell might consist of two pieces of metal, one zinc and the other copper, each immersed each in a solution containing a dissolved salt of the corresponding metal. The two solutions are separated by a porous barrier that prevents them from rapidly mixing but allows ions to diffuse through.If we simply left it at that, no significant amount of reaction would take place. However, if we connect the zinc and copper by means of a metallic conductor, the excess electrons that remain when Zn^{2+} ions go into solution in the left cell would be able to flow through the external circuit and into the right electrode, where they could be delivered to the Cu^{2+} ions which become "*discharged*", that is, converted into Cu atoms at the surface of the copper electrode. The net reaction is the same as before— the oxidation of zinc by copper(II) ions: $Zn(s) + Cu^{2+} \rightarrow Zn^{2+} + Cu(s)$ but this time, the oxidation and reduction steps take place in separate locations: *left electrode:* $Zn(s) \rightarrow Zn^{2+} + 2e^-$ *oxidation right electrode:* $Cu^{2+} + 2e^- \rightarrow Cu(s)$ *reduction* Electrochemical cells allow measurement and control of a redox reaction. The reaction can be started and stopped by connecting or disconnecting the two electrodes. If we place a variable resistance in the circuit, we can even control the rate of the net cell reaction by simply turning a knob. By connecting a battery or other source of current to the two electrodes, we can force the reaction to proceed in its non-spontaneous, or *reverse* direction.

By placing an ammeter in the external circuit, we can measure the amount of electric charge that passes through the electrodes, and thus the number of moles of reactants that get

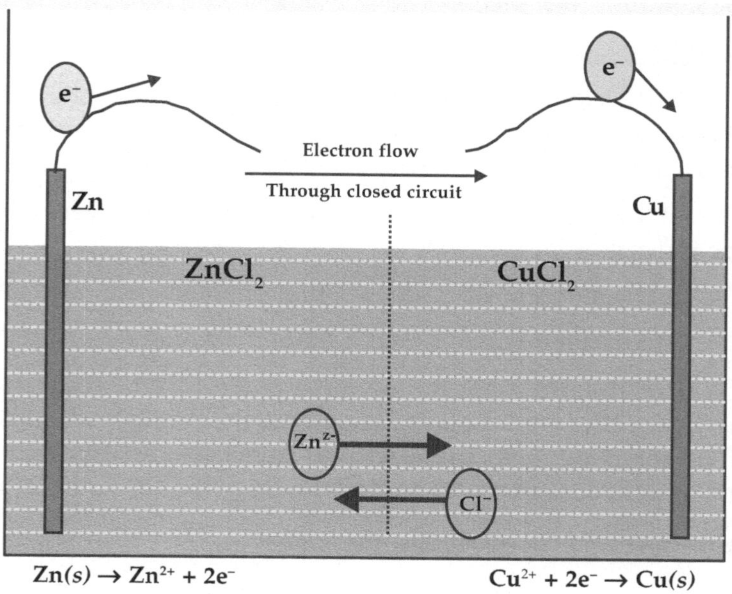

Fig. 3.1: **A Simple Electrochemical cell**

transformed into products in the cell reaction. Electric charge q is measured in coulombs. The amount of charge carried by one mole of electrons is known as the *faraday*, which we denote by F. Careful experiments have determined that 1 F = 96467 c. For most purposes, you can simply use 96,500 coulombs as the value of the faraday.

The two compartments of this cell are separated by a porous barrier that allows ions to pass through while preventing gross mixing of the two solutions. When the two electrodes are connected, charges flow in the directions indicated. Note thatthe buildup of positive charge on the left side can be offset either by diffusionof Zn^{2+} to the right or (less efficiently) by Cl^- to the left.

When we measure electric current, we are measuring the rate at which electric charge is transported through the circuit. A current of one ampere corresponds to the flow of one coulomb per second.

Problem Example 1:

In the cell of Fig. 3.1, how much mass would the zinc electrode lose if a current of 0.15 amp flows through the external circuit for 1.5 hours?

Soution. The amount of charge passing between the electrodes is

(0.15 amp) × (54600 sec) = 810 c or

(810 c)/(96500 c F–1) = 0.0084 F

Sinc the oxidation of one mole of Zn to Zn^{2+} results in the removal of two moles of electrons, the number of moles of Zn removed from the electrode is 0.0042, corresponding to a weight loss of (.0043 mol) × (65.37 g mol–1) = 0.275 g

Transport of Charge within the Cell

In order for the cell of Fig. 3.1 to operate, not only must there be an external electrical circuit between the two electrodes, but the two electrolytes (the solutions) must be in contact. The need for this can be understood by considering what happens to the two solutions as the cell reaction proceeds. Positive charge (in the form of Zn^{2+}) is added to the electrolyte in the left compartment, and removed (as Cu^{2+}) from the right side, causing the solution in contact with the zinc to acquire a net positive charge, while a net negative charge would build up in the solution on the copper side of the cell. These violations of electroneutrality would make it more difficult (require more work) to introduce additional Zn2+ ions into the positivelycharged electrolyte or for electrons to flow into right compartment where they are needed to reduce the Cu2+ ions, thus effectively stopping the reaction after only a minute amount has taken place.

In order to sustain the cell reaction, the charge carried by the electrons through the external circuit must be accompanied by a compensating transport of ions between the two cells. This means that we must provide a path for ions to move directly from one cell to the other. This ionic transport involves not only the electroactive species Cu^{2+} and Zn^{2+}, but also the counterions, which in this example are NO3–. Thus an excess of Cu^{2+} in the left compartment could be alleviated by the drift of these ions into the right side, or equally well by diffusion of nitrate ions to the left. More detailed studies reveal that both processes occur, and that the relative amounts of charge carried through the solution by positive and negative ions depends on their relative *mobilities*, which express the velocity with which the ions are able to make their way through the solution. Since negative ions tend to be larger than positive ions, the latter tend to have higher mobilities and carry the larger fraction of charge.

In the simplest cells, the barrier between the two solutions can be a porous membrane, but for precise measurements, a more complicated arrangement, known as a salt bridge, is used. The salt bridge consists of an intermediate compartment filled with a concentrated solution of KCl and fitted with porous barriers at each end. The purpose of the salt bridge is to minimize the natural potential difference, known as the *junction potential,* that develops (as mentioned in the previous section) when any two phases (such as the two solutions) are in contact. This potential difference would combine with the two half-cell potentials so as introduce a degree of uncertainty into any measurement of the cell potential.

As a matter of convention, the chemical species that undergo reduction when the cell reaction proceeds to the right according to the net equation are shown on the right side, and those that undergo oxidation are shown on the left. Note carefully that this is entirely independent of the physical location of the two electrodes in the actual cell. There are several other conventions relating to cell notation and nomenclature that you are expected to know:

- The *anode* is where oxidation occurs, and the *cathode* is the site of reduction. In an actual cell, either electrode can have either identity, depending on the direction in which the net cell reaction is occurring.
- If electrons flow from the left electrode to the right electrode (as depicted in the above cell notation) when the cell operates in its spontaneous direction, the potential of the right electrode will be higher than that of the left, and the *cell potential* will be *positive.*
- "Conventional current flow" is from positive to negative, which is opposite to the direction of the electron flow. This means that if the electrons are flowing from the left electrode to the right, a galvanometer placed in the external circuit would indicate a current flow from right to left.

Electrodes and Electrode Reactions

The electron-transfer step that takes place at each electrode is known as the *electrode reaction*.

The substances that receive and lose electrons are called the *electroactive species*.

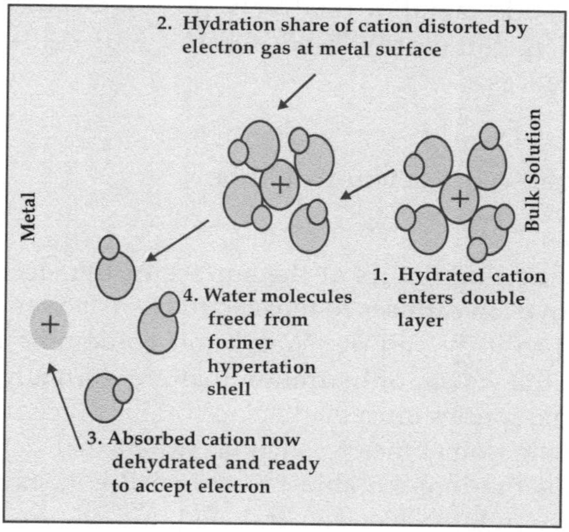

Fig. 3.2: **Electron transfer at an electrode**

This process takes place within the very thin interfacial region at the electrode surface, and involves quantum-mechanical tunneling of electrons between the electrode and the electroactive species. The work required to displace the H_2O molecules in the hydration spheres of the ions constitutes part of the activation energy of the process.

In the example of the Zn/Cu cell we have been using, the electrode reaction involves a metal and its hydrated cation; we call such electrodes metal-metal ion electrodes. There are a number of other kinds of electrodes which are widely encountered in electrochemistry and analytical chemistry.

Ion-ion Electrodes

Many electrode reactions involve only ionic species, such as Fe^{2+} and Fe^{3+}. If neither of the electroactive species is a metal, some other metal must serve as a conduit for the supply or removal of electrons from the system. In order to avoid complications that would arise from electrode reactions involving this metal, a relatively inert substance such as platinum is commonly used. Such a half cell would be represented as:

$$Pt(s) \mid Fe_{(ab)} \mid\mid \ldots$$

and the half-cell reaction would be

$$Fe^{2+}_{(ab)} \rightarrow Fe^{3+}_{(ab)} + e^{-}$$

The reaction occurs at the surface of the electrode The electroactive ion diffuses to the electrode surface and adsorbs (attaches) to it by van der Waals and coulombic forces. In doing so, the waters of hydration that are normally attached to any ionic species must be displaced. This process is always endothermic, sometimes to such an extent that only a small fraction of the ions be able to contact the surface closely enough to undergo electron transfer, and the reaction will be slow. The actual electron-transfer occurs by quantum-mechanical *tunnelling*.

Gas Electrodes

Some electrode reactions involve a gaseous species such as H_2, O_2, or Cl_2. Such reactions must also be carried out on the surface of an electrochemically inert conductor such as platinum.

Although the usefulness of such an electrode may not be immediately apparent, this kind of electrode finds very wide application in electrochemical measurements, as we shall see later.

Standard Half-cell Potentials

When a net reaction proceeds in an electrochemical cell, oxidation occurs at one electrode (the anode) and reduction takes place at the other electrode (the cathode.) We can think of the cell as consisting of two *half-cells* joined together by an external circuit through which electrons flow and an internal pathway that allows ions to migrate between them so as to preserve electroneutrality.

Reduction Potentials

Each half-cell has associated with it a potential difference whose magnitude depends on the nature of the particular electrode reaction and on the concentrations of the dissolved electroactive species. The *sign* of this potential difference depends on the direction (oxidation or reduction) in which the electrode reaction proceeds. In order express them in a uniform way, we adopt the convention that half-cell potentials are always defined for the *reduction* direction. Thus the half-cell potential for the Zn/Zn^{2+} electrode (or *couple* as it is sometimes called) is defined as the potential difference between a piece of metallic zinc and the solution when the reaction:

$$Zn^{2+} + 2e^{-} \rightarrow Zn(s)$$

takes place. In the cell

$$Zn(s) \mid Zn^{2+}_{(ab)} \mid\mid Cu^{2+}_{(ab)} \mid Cu(s)$$

the zinc appears on the left side, indicating that it is being oxidized, not reduced. For this reason, the potential difference contributed by the left half-cell has the opposite sign to its conventional half-cell potential. More generally, we can define the *cell potential* or *cell EMF* as Ecell = DV = Eright – Eleft in which "right" and "left" refer to the cell notation convention ("reduction on the right") and not, of course, to the physical orientation of a real cell in the laboratory. If we expand the above expression we see that the cell potential Ecell = VCu – Vsoln + Vsoln – VZn is just the *difference* between the two half-cell potentials Eright and Eleft.

Reference Half-cells

The fact that individual half-cell potentials are not directly measurable does not prevent us from defining and working with them. Although we cannot determine the absolute value of a half-cell potential, we can still measure its value in relation to the potentials of other half cells. In particular, if we adopt a reference half-cell whose potential is arbitrarily defined as zero, and measure the potentials of various other electrode systems against this reference cell, we are in effect measuring the half-cell potentials on a scale that is relative to the potential of the reference cell.

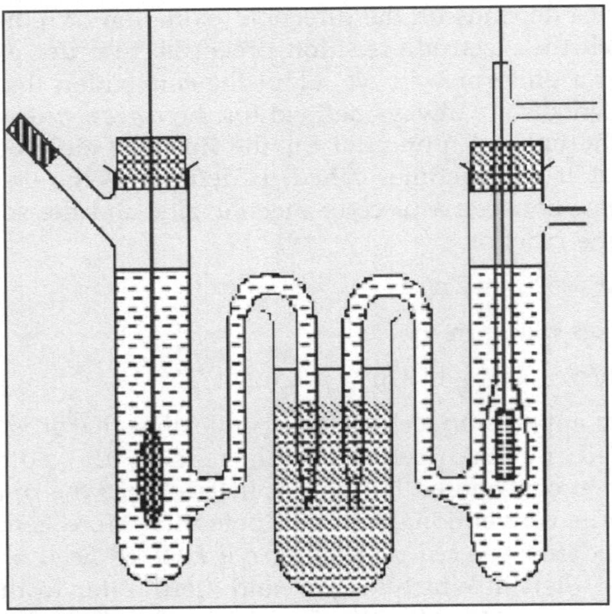

Fig. 3.3: **Measurement of standard potenitals**

The hydrogen reference electrode is shown the electrode system being measured is on the left. The two halfcells are joined by a salt bridge.

Standard potentials for hundreds of electrodes have been determined (mostly in the period 1925-45, during which time they were referred to as "oxidation potentials") and are usually tabulated in order of increasing tendency to accept electrons. This ordering is also known as the "electromotive series of the elements." As can be seen in the abbreviated version in Table 3.1, sodium is the most "active" of the metallic elements in the sense that its oxidation product Na+ shows the smallest tendency (as indicated by the highly negative voltage) to undergo reduction.

Table 3.1: Some standard reduction potentials

Oxidant (electron acceptor)	Reductant (electron donor)	Volts
Na^{+}	Na(s)	−2.71 v
Zn^{2+}	Zn(s)	−.76
Fe^{2+}	Fe(s)	−.44
Cd^{2+}	Cd(s)	−.40
Pb^{2+}	Pb(s)	−.126
2 H^{+}	H2(g)	0.000
AgCl(s)	Ag(s) + Cl−(aq)	+.222
Hg2Cl2(s)	2 Cl−(aq) + Hg(l)	+.268
$Cu2^{+}$	Cu(s)	+.337
I2(s)	2 I−	+.535
$Fe3^{+}$	Fe^{2+}	+.771
Ag^{+}	Ag(s)	+.799
O2(g) + 4 H^{+}	2 H_2O(l)	+1.23
Cl2(g)	2 Cl^{-}	+1.36

These couples (an oxidant and its conjugate reductant) are arranged in order of increasing tendency of the species in the leftmost column (oxidizing agents) to accept electrons. Each of the metals (center column) is able to donate electrons to (reduce) any oxidant below it. The elements that appear above H2 are called *active metals* because they are able to react with acids, reducing H+ to H2. Notice that chlorine gas is able to remove electrons from (oxidize) water.

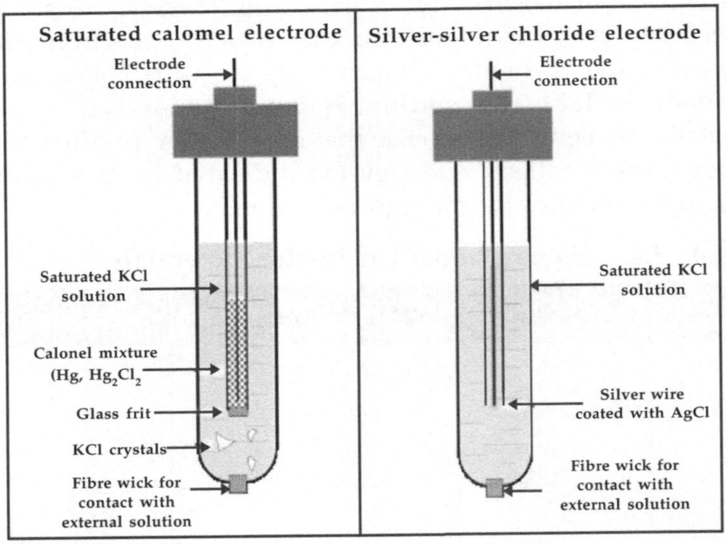

Fig. 3.4: **Reference electrodes: the silver-silver chloride and calomel electrodes**

Reference Electrodes

In most electrochemical experiments our interest is concentrated on only one of the electrode reactions. Since all measurements must be on a complete cell involving two electrode systems, it is common practice to employ a reference electrode as the other half of the cell. The major requirements of a reference electrode are that it be easy to prepare and maintain, and that its potential be stable. The last requirement essentially means that the concentration of any ionic species involved in the electrode reaction must be held at a fixed value. The most common way of accomplishing this is to use an electrode reaction involving a saturated solution of an insoluble salt of the ion. One such system, the silver-silver chloride electrode has already been mentioned.

This electrode usually takes the form of a piece of silver wire coated with AgCl. The coating is done by making the silver the anode in an electrolytic cell containing HCl; the Ag^+ ions combine with Cl^- ions as fast as they are formed at the silver surface.

The other common reference electrode is the calomel electrode; calomel is the common name for mercury(I) chloride.

The potentials of both of these electrodes have been very accurately determined against the hydrogen electrode. The latter is seldom used in routine electrochemical measurements because it is more difficult to prepare; the platinum surface has to be specially treated by preliminary electrolysis. Also, there is need for a supply of hydrogen gas which makes it somewhat cumbersome and hazardous.

Prediction and Significance of Cell Potentials

Given the values for two half reactions, you can easily predict the potential difference of the corresponding cell: simply add the reduction potential of the reduction half-cell to the negative of the reduction potential (that is, to the oxidation potential) of the oxidation reaction.

Since this potential is positive, tthe reaction will proceed to the right; electrons will be withdrawn from the copper electrode and flow through the external circuit into the silver electrode. Note carefully that in combining these half-cell potentials, we did not multiply E° the for the Cu^{2+}/Cu couple by two. The reason for this will be explained later.

Cell Potentials and the Electromotive Series

Tables containing the same sequence of reactions as in Table 3.1, but without the voltage data, were in common use long before electrochemical cells were studied and half-cell potentials had been measured. If you read down the central column, you will notice that it begins with the sequence of metals Na, Zn, Fe, etc. This sequence is known as the *activity series of the metals*, and expresses the decreasing tendency these species to lose electrons- that is, to undergo oxidation.

The activity series has long been used to predict the direction of oxidation-reduction reactions. Consider, for example, the oxidation of Cu by metallic zinc that we have mentioned previously. The fact that zinc is near the top of the activity series means that this metal has to lose electrons. By the same token, the tendency of Zn to accept electrons is relatively small. Copper, on the other hand, is a poorer electron donor, and thus its oxidized form, Cu, is a fairly good electron acceptor. We would therefore expect the reaction.

$$Zn(s) + Cu^{2+} \rightarrow Zn^{2+} + Cu(s)$$

to proceed in the direction indicated, rather than in the reverse direction. An old-fashioned way of expressing this is to say that "zinc will displace copper from solution". The half-cell potentials listed in Table 1enable us to attach numbers to our predictions. As was implied in the preceding problem example, if the potential of a cell made up of the two half-cell reactions is positive, then the reaction will proceed spontaneously to the right; if it is negative, the reverse reaction will be spontaneous.

Cell Potentials and Free Energy

From the above, it should be apparent that the potential difference between the electrodes of a cell is a measure of the tendency for the cell reaction to take place: the more positive the cell potential, the greater the tendency for the reaction to proceed to the right. But we already know that the standard free energy change, expresses the tendency for any kind of process to occur under the conditions of constant temperature and pressure. Thus and measure the same thing, and are related in a simple way:

$$\Delta G^{o} = -nFE^{o}$$

A few remarks are in order about this very fundamental and important relation:

- The negative sign on the right indicates that a positive cell potential (according to the sign convention discussed previously) implies a negative free energy change, and thus that the cell reaction will proceed to the right.
- Electrical work is done when an electric charge q moves through a potential difference DV. It refers to the movement of n moles of charge across the cell potential E^o, and thus has the dimensions of work.
- The value of DG° expresses the *maximum useful work* that a system can do on the surroundings.

"Useful" work is that which can be extracted from the cell by electrical means to operate a lamp or some other external device. This excludes any P-V work that is simply a consequence of volume change (which could of course conceivably be put to some use!) and which would be performed in any case, even if the reactants were combined directly. This quantity of work – DG° can only be extracted from the system under the limiting conditions of a reversible change, which for an electrochemical cell implies zero current. The more rapidly the cell operates, the less electrical work it can supply. If F is expressed in coulombs per mole, the electrical work is in joules per mole. To relate these units to electrical units, recall that the coulomb is one amp-sec, and that power, which is the rate at which work is done, is measured in watts, which is the product of amps and volts.

The Fall of the Electron

A table of standard half-cell potentials such as in Table 3.1 summarizes a large amount of chemistry, for it expresses the relative powers of various substances to donate and accept electrons by listing reduction half-reactions in order of increasing E^o values, and thus of increasing spontaneity. The greater the value of E^o, the greater the tendency of the substance on the left to acquire electrons, and thus the stronger this substance is as an oxidizing agent. One can draw a useful analogy between acid-base and oxidation-reduction reactions. Both involve the transfer of a species from a source, the donor, to a sink, the acceptor. The source and sink nomenclature implies that the tendency of the proton (in the case of acids) or of the electron (for reducing agents) to undergo transfer is proportional to the fall in free energy. From the relation DG° = RT ln Ka, you can see that the acid dissociation constant is a measure of the fall in free energy of the proton when it is transferred from a donor HA to the solvent H_2O, which represents the reference (zero) free energy level of the proton in aqueous solution.

In the same way, a standard half-cell potential is a measure of the drop in the free energy of the electron when it "falls" from its source level to the energy of the hydrogen ion at unit effective concentration. By virtue of the defined value of $E^o = 0$ for the H^+/H^2 couple, the latter level can also be regarded as the zero free energy level of the electron.

- For example, it is seen that Fe^{3+}, representing a rather low-lying empty level, can accept electrons from, and thus oxidize, I^-, Cu(s), or any higher reductant. Similarly, if and Fe^{3+} and I^- 3 are both present, one would expect a higher reductant to preferentially reduce Fe^{3+}, as long the two reductions take place at similar rates.

- Water can undergo both oxidation and reduction. In the latter role, water can serve as an electron sink to any metal listed above it. These metals are all thermodynamically unstable in the presence of water. A spectacular example of this is the action of water on metallic sodium.

- Water can donate electrons to any acceptor below it. For example, an aqueous solution of Cl^2 will decompose into hypochlorous acid (HOCl) with the evolution of oxygen. (Note, however, that this reaction is extremely slow in the absence of light.)

- Only those substances that appear between the two reactions involving water will be stable in aqueous solution in both their oxidized and reduced forms. A metal that is above the H^+/H^2 couple will react with acids, liberating H^2; these are sometimes known as the "active" metals. Such metals will also of course react with water, although often at a very small rate.

Fig. 3.5 Electron free energy diagram for aqueous solution This diagram contains the same information as a table of standard potentials, but its different arrangement can provide more insight into the meaning of E° values. The vertical axis indicates the free energies of electron when attached to various species, relative to that of the electron in H^2. The scale on the left expresses the E° values; i.e. as free energies per electron-mole. The scale on the right shows the same thing in terms of kJ.

The chemical species shown on the left are oxidants (oxidizing agents) which can be regarded as possessing vacant electron-free energy levels. A redox reaction will be spontaneous only if the reductant ("electron source" in the table) is located above that of the desired "electron sink". The similarity between this table and a table of proton free energies is striking; just as the pH defines the average proton free energy in a solution and thus controls the ratio of conjugate acid and base, so does the E° control the ratio of conjugate oxidant and reductant concentrations. There is, however, one very important difference: proton-exchange reactions are very fast, so if several different bases (proton sinks) are available in the same solution, they get filled from the bottom up. Redox reactions, in contrast, can be extremely slow. This means that an energetically-allowed electron transfer may not occur at an observable rate, and the outcome of an electron transfer when several oxidants are

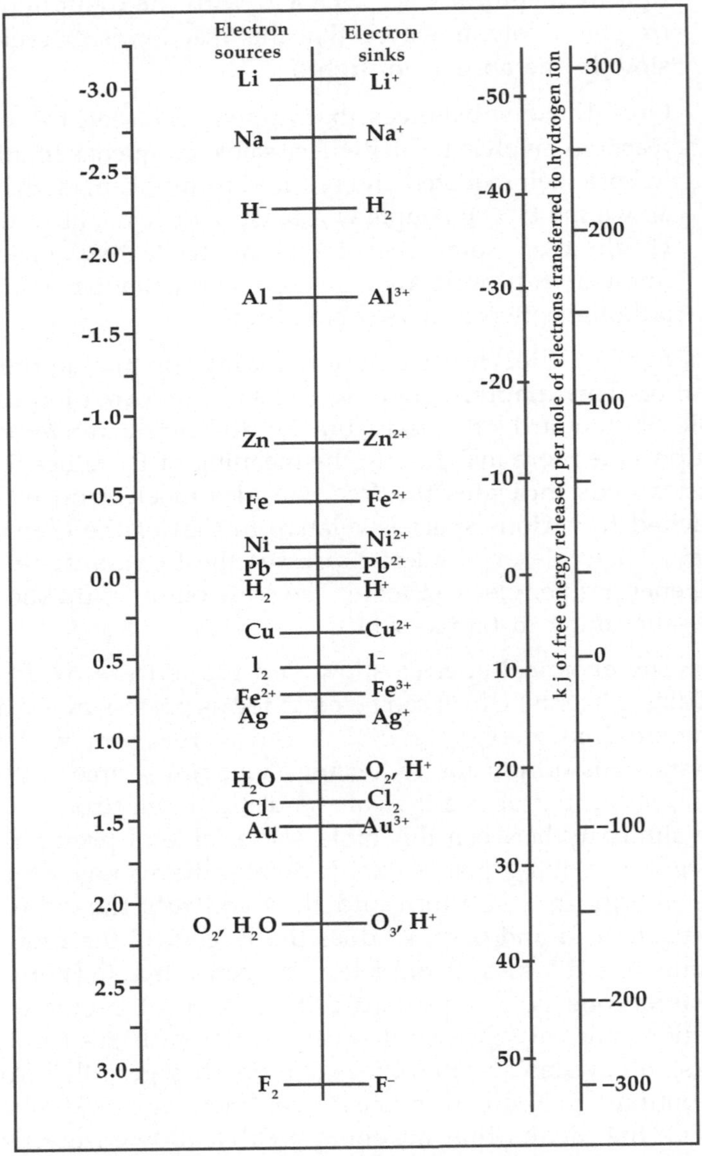

Fig. 3.5: **Electron free energy diagram**

present in the same solution will be decided by kinetics rather than by thermodynamics. This explains why Cl^2, for example does not ordinarily reduce (i.e., decompose) H_2O, or why Pb is relatively inert to acids.

Latimer Diagrams

Considerable insight into the chemistry of a single element can be had by comparing the standard electrode potentials (and thus the relative free energies) of the various oxidation states of the element. The most convenient means of doing this is the Latimer diagram.

Oxidation state	**+ 6**		**+ 3**		**+ 2**		**O**
Acid solution	FeO_4^{2-}	+1.9	Fe^{3+}	+.771	Fe^{2+}	-.440	Fe
Alkaline solution	FeO_4^{2-}	+.9	$Fe(OH)_3$	-.56	$Fe(OH)_2$	-.89	Fe

Oxidation	**+6**		**+4**		**+2**		**+1**		**0**		**-1**
Acid solution	ClO_4^-	+1.19	ClO_3^-	+1.21	ClO_2^-	+1.64	HClO	+1.63	Cl_2	+1.35	Cl^-
Alkaline solution	ClO_4^-	+.36	ClO_3^-	+.33	ClO_2^-	+.66	ClO^-	+.40	Cl_2	+1.35	Cl^-

Fig. 3.6: **Latimer diagrams**

The formulas of the species that represent each oxidation state of the element are written from left to right in order of decreasing oxidation number, and the standard potential for the reduction of each species to the next on the right is written in between the formulas. Potentials for reactions involving hydrogen ions will be pH dependent so separate diagrams are usually provided for acidic and alkaline solutions (effective hydrogen ion concentrations of 1M and 10^{-14} M, respectively).

The more positive the reduction potential, the greater will be the tendency of the species on the left to be reduced to the one on the right. To see how Latimer diagrams are used, look first at the one for iron in acid solution. The line connecting Fe^{3+} and Fe^{2+} represents the reaction:

$$Fe^{3+} + e^{-} \rightarrow Fe^{2+}$$

whose positive E^{o} (.440 v) indicates that metallic iron will dissolve in acidic solution to form Fe2+. Because the oxidation of this species to the +3 state has a negative potential (.771v; moving to the left on the diagram reverses the sign), the +2 state will be the stable oxidation state of iron under these conditions.

Disproportionation

An important condition to recognize is when the potential on the left of a species is less positive than that on the right. This indicates that the species can oxidize and reduce *itself*, a process known as *disproportionation*. As an example, consider Cl^{2} in alkaline solution. The potential for its reduction to Cl^{-} is sufficiently positive (+1.35 v) to supply the free energy necessary for the oxidation of one atom of chlorine to hypochlorite. Thus elemental chlorine is thermodynamically unstable with respect to disproportionation in alkaline solution, and the same it true of the oxidation product, $HClO^{-}$.

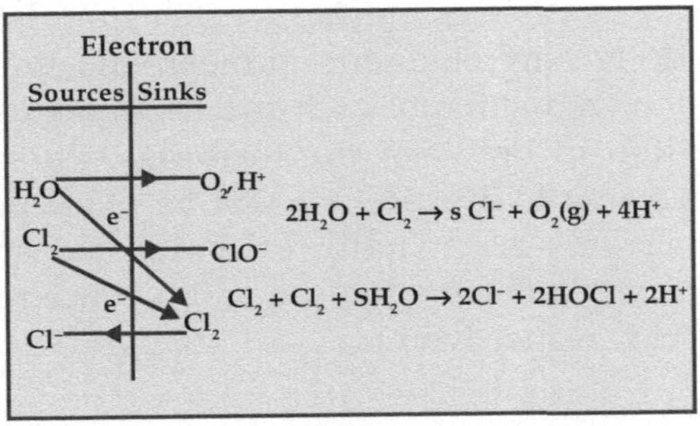

Fig. 3.7: **Behaviour of chlorine in water**

Cl_2 can oxidize water (top) and also undergo disproportionation (bot om). In the latter process, one Cl_2 molecule donates electrons to another.

Bear in mind that many oxidation-reduction reactions, unlike most acid-base reactions, tend to be very slow, so the fact that a species is thermodynamically unstable does not always mean that it will quickly decompose. Thus the two reactions shown in the figure are normally very slow.

The Nernst Equation

The standard cell potentials we have been discussing refer to cells in which all dissolved substances are at unit activity, which essentially means an "effective concentration" of 1*M*. Similarly, any gases that take part in an electrode reaction are at an effective pressure (known as the *fugacity*) of 1 atm. If these concentrations or pressures have other values, the cell potential will change in a manner that can be predicted from the principles you already know. Suppose, for example, that we reduce the concentration of Zn2+ in the Zn/Cu cell from its standard effective value of 1*M* to an to a much smaller value:

$$Zn(s) \mid Zn^{2+}_{(aq)}, .001M) \mid\mid Cu^{2+}_{(aq)} \mid Cu(s)$$

This will reduce the value of *Q* for the cell reaction

$$Zn(s) + Cu^{2+} \rightleftharpoons Zn^{2+} + Cu(s)$$

thus making it more spontaneous, or "driving it to the right" as the Le Châtelier principle would predict, and making its free energy change DG more negative than DG°, so that *E* would be more positive than *E*°. The relation between the actual cell potential *E* and the standard potential *E*° is developed in the following way. We begin with Eq. 10 which relates the standard free energy change (for the complete conversion of products into reactants) to the standard potential

$$DG^{\circ} = -nFE^{\circ}$$

By analogy we can write the more general equation

$$DG = -nFE$$

which expresses the change in free energy for any extent of reaction— that is, for any value of the reaction quotient Q. We now substitute these into the expression that relates DG and DG° which you will recall from the chapter on chemical equilibrium:

$$DG = DG^{o} + RT \ln Q$$

which gives

$$-nFE = -nFE^{o} + RT \ln Q$$

which can be rearranged to

$$E = E^{o} - \frac{RT}{nF} \ln Q$$

This is the very important *Nernst equation* which relates the cell potential to the standard potential and to the activities of the electroactive species. Notice that the cell potential will be the same as E^{o} only if Q is unity. The Nernst equation is more commonly written in base-10 log form and for 25°C:

$$E = E^{o} - \frac{0.059}{n} \log Q$$

Significance of the Nernst Equation

This relation tells us that a cell potential will change by 59 millivolts per 10-fold change in the concentration of a substance involved in a one-electron oxidation or reduction; for twoelectron processes, the variation will be 28 millivolts per decade concentration change. Thus for the dissolution of metallic copper

$$Cu(s) \rightleftharpoons Cu^{2+} + 2e^{-}$$

the potential

$$E = 0.337 - .0295 \log [Cu^{2+}]$$

becomes more positive (the reaction has a greater tendency to take place) as the cupric ion concentrated decreases. This, of course, is exactly what the Le Châtelier Principle predicts; the more dilute the product, the greater the extent of the reaction.

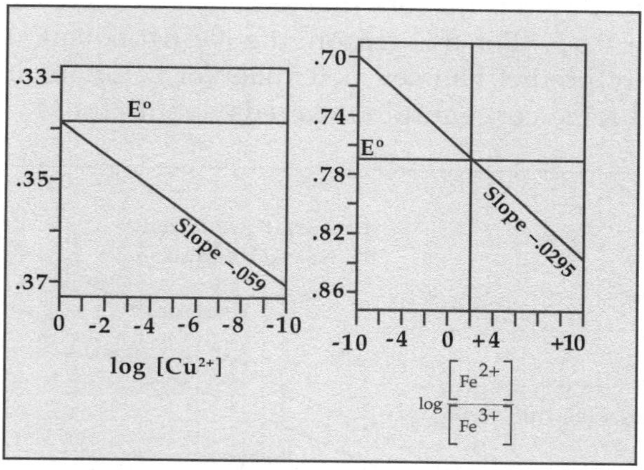

Fig. 3.8: **Plots of the Nernst Equation**

Electrodes with Poise

This raises an interesting question: suppose you immerse a piece of copper in a solution of pure water. With $Q = [Cu^{2+}] = 0$, the potential difference between the electrode and the solution should be infinite! Are you in danger of being electrocuted? You need not worry; without any electron transfer, there is no charge to zap you with. Of course it won't be very long before some Cu^{2+} ions appear in the solution, and if there are only a few such ions per liter, the potential reduces to only about 20 volts. More to the point, however, the system is so far from equilibrium (for example, there are not enough ions to populate the electric double layer) that the Nernst equation doesn't really give meaningful results. Such an electrode is said to be un*poised*. What ionic concentration is needed to poise an electrode? I don't really know, but I would be suspicious of anything much below 10^{-6} *M*.

The Nernst Equation Works only in *dilute* Ionic Solutions

Ions of opposite charge tend to associate into loosely-bound *ion pairs* in more concentrated solutions, thus reducing the number of ions that are free to donate or accept electrons at an electrode. For this reason, the Nernst equation cannot accurately predict half-cell potentials for solutions in which the total ionic concentration exceeds about 10^{-3} *M*.

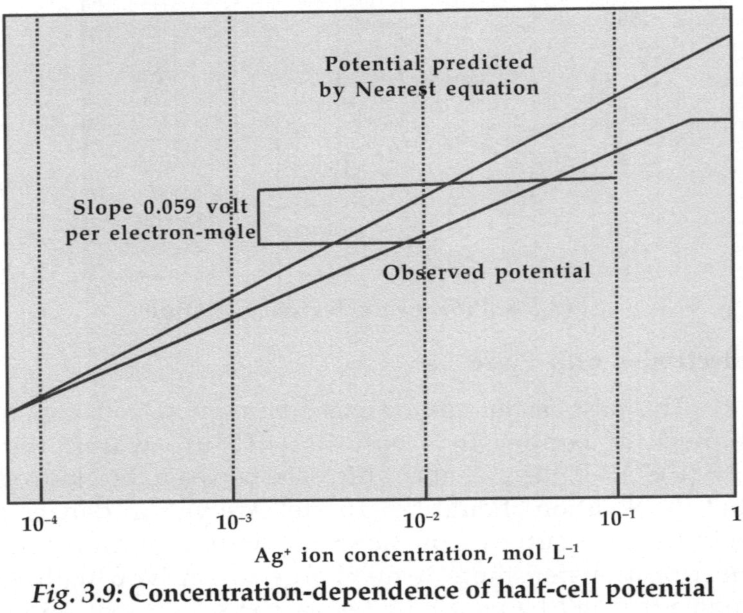

Fig. 3.9: **Concentration-dependence of half-cell potential**

The Nernst Equation accurately predicts half-cell potentials only when the equilibrium quotient term Q is expressed in activities. Ionic activities depart increasingly from concentrations when the latter exceed 10^{-4} - 10^{-3} M, depending on the size and charge of the ion.

Activities and Activity Coefficients

If the Nernst equation is applied to more concentrated solutions, the terms in the reaction quotient Q must be expressed in "effective concentrations" or *activities* of the electroactive ionic species. The *activity coefficient* γ (gamma) relates the concentration of an ion to its activity a in a given solution through the relation.

$$a = \gamma c$$

Since electrode potentials measure activities directly, activity coefficients can be determined by carrying out appropriate EMF measurements on cells in which the concentration of the ion of interest is known. The resulting *E*s can then be used to convert concentrations into activities for use in other calculations involving equilibrium constants.

Cell Potentials and pH; Stability Diagrams

As most of us recall from our struggles with balancing redox equations in our beginning chemistry courses, many electron-transfer reactions involve hydrogen ions and hydroxide ions. The standard potentials for these reactions, therefore refer to the pH, either 0 or 14, at which the appropriate ion has unit activity. Because multiple numbers of H^+ or OH^- ions are often involved, the potentials given by the Nernst equation can vary greatly with the pH.

It is frequently useful to look at the situation in another way by considering what combinations of potential and pH allow the stable existence of a particular species. This information is most usefully expressed by means of a *E-vs.-pH* diagram, also known as a *Pourbaix* diagram.

Stability of Water

As was noted in connection with the shaded region in Fig. 3.7, water is subject to decomposition by strong oxidizing agents such as Cl^2 and by reducing agents stronger than H^2. The reduction reaction can be written either as:

$2H^+ + 2e^- \rightarrow H^2(g)$

or, in neutral or alkaline solutions as

$H_2O + 2e^- \rightarrow H^2(g) + 2\ OH^-$

These two reactions are equivalent and follow the same Nernst equation

$$E_H + lH_1 = E^o{}_{H^+/H_1} + \frac{RT}{nF}\ln\frac{[H^+]^2}{p_{H1}}$$

which, at 25°C and unit H^2 partial pressure reduces to

$$E = E^o - 0.059\ pH = -0.059\ pH$$

Similarly, the oxidation of water

$$H_2O \rightarrow O^2(g) + 4\ H^+ + 2e^-$$

is governed by the Nernst equation

$$E_{O_2/H_2O} = E^0{}_{O_1/H_1O} + \frac{RT}{nF}\ln p_{o_1}.[H^+]^4$$

From this information we can construct the stability diagram for water shown below (Fig. 3.10).

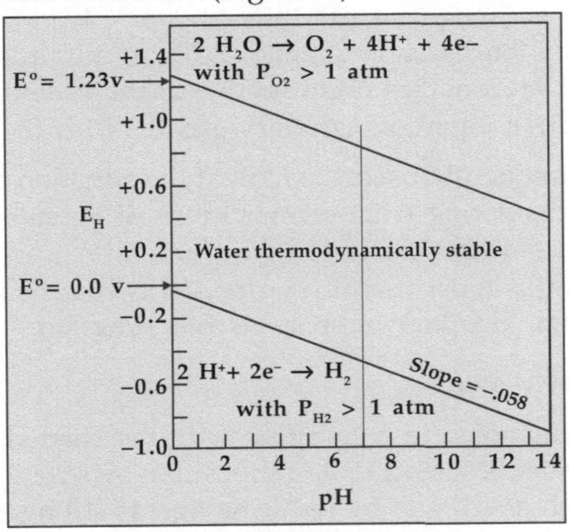

Fig. 3.10: **Stability diagram**

Fig. 3.10 Stability (Pourbaix) diagram for water This diagram has special relevance to electrochemical corrosion Thus metals above H² in activity series will tend to undergo oxidation (corrosion) by reducing H^+ ions or water. The unity partial pressures are of course purely arbitrary criteria; in a system open to the atmosphere, water can decompose even at much lower hydrogen partial pressures.

Chlorine in Water

Because chlorine is widely used as a disinfectant for drinking water, swimming pools, and sewage treatment, it is worth looking at its stability (Fig. 3.11).

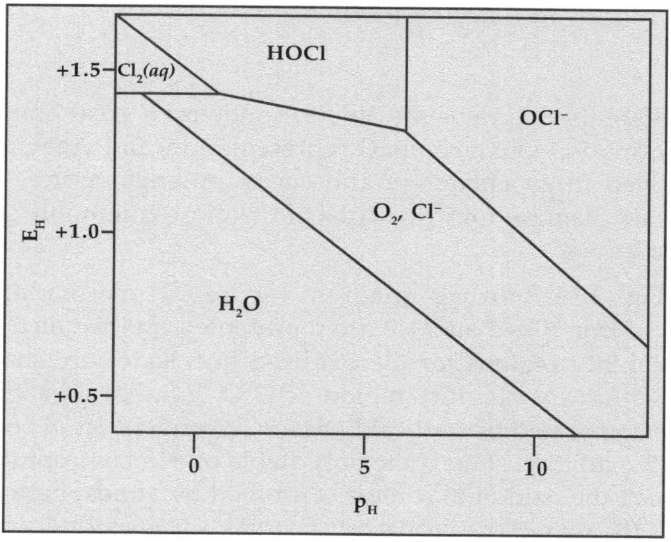

Fig. 3.11: **Stability diagram for chlorine in water Equilibria between species separated by diagonal lines are dependent on both E and pH, while those separated by horizontal or vertical lines are affected by pH only or E only, respectively**

Note that the effective bactericidal agent is not Cl² itself, but its oxidation product hypochlorous acid HOCl which predominates at pH values below its pKa of 7.3. Note also that:

- Cl_2 is unstable except at very low pH; it decomposes into HOCl and Cl^-.
- Hypochlorous acid and its anion are stronger oxidants than O_2 and thus subject to decomposition in water. The only stable chlorine species in water is Cl^-.
- Decomposition of HOCl occurs very slowly in the dark, but is catalyzed by sunlight. For this reason the chlorine in outside swimming pools must be frequently renewed.
- Decomposition of Cl^2 and HOCl by reaction with organic material in municipal water supply systems sometimes makes it necessary to inject additional chlorine at outlying locations.

Iron

Stability diagrams are able to condense a great amount of information into a compact representation, and are widely employed in geochemistry and corrosion engineering. The Pourbaix diagram for iron is one of the more commonly seen examples.

Fig. 3.12 Pourbaix diagram for iron Three oxidation states of iron (0, +2 and +3) are represented on this diagram. The stability regions for the oxidized iron states are shown only within the stability region of H_2O. Equilibria between species separated by vertical lines are dependent on pH only. The +3 oxidation state is the only stable one in environments in which the oxidation level is controlled by atmospheric O_2. This is the reason the Earths crust contains iron oxides, which developed only after the appearance of green plants which are the source of O_2. Iron is attacked by H+ to form H_2 and Fe(II); the latter then reacts with O_2 to form the various colored Fe(III) oxides that constitute "rust". Numerous other species such as oxides and hydrous oxides are not shown. A really "complete" diagram for iron would need to have at least two additional dimensions showing the partial pressures of O_2 and CO_2.

Concentration Cells

From your study of thermodynamics you may recall that the process solute *(concentrated)* ® solute *(dilute)* is accompanied by a fall in free energy, and therefore is capable of doing work on the surroundings; all that is required is some practical way of capturing this work. One way of oing this is by means of a *concentration cell* such as:

$$Cu(s) \mid CuNO_3(.1\,M) \mid\mid CuNO_3(.01\,M) \mid Cu(s)$$

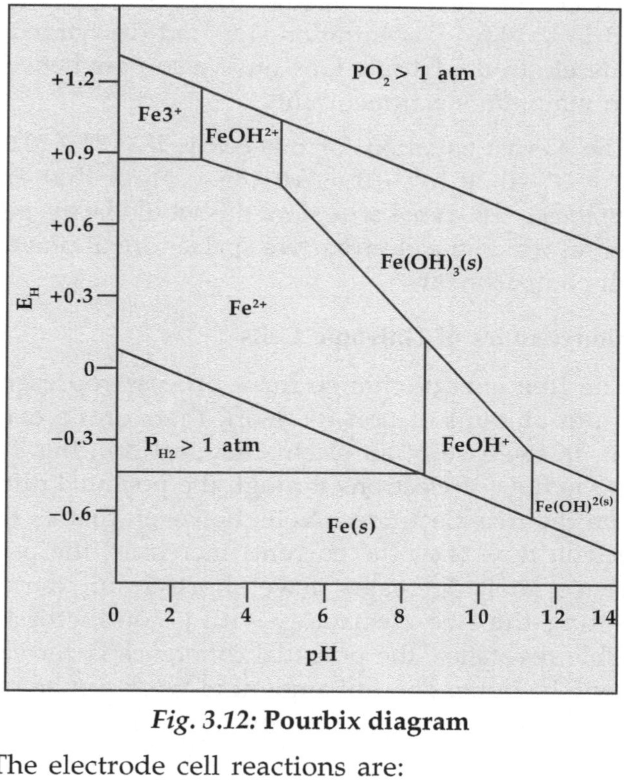

Fig. 3.12: **Pourbix diagram**

The electrode cell reactions are:

cathode: $Cu^{2+}(.1\,M) + 2e^- \rightarrow Cu(s)$

anode: $Cu(s) \rightarrow Cu^{2+}(.01\,M) + 2e^-$

net: $Cu^{2+}(.1\,M) \rightarrow Cu^{2+}(.01\,M)$

which represents the transport of cupric ion from a region of higher concentration to one of lower concentration. The driving force for this process is the free energy change DG associated with the concentration gradient ($C2 - C1$), sometimes known as the *free energy of dilution*:

$$\Delta Gdilution = RT\ ln(C2/C1)$$

Note, however, that Cu^{2+} ions need not physically move between the two compartments; electron flow through the external circuit creates a "virtual" flow as copper ions are created in the low-concentration side and discharged at the opposite electrode. Nitrate ions must also pass between the cells to maintain electroneutrality.

The Nernst equation for this cell is $E = E^o - (0.059/N) \log Q = 0 - 0.29 \log 0.1 = +0.285$ v Note that E^o *for a concentration cell is always zero*, since this would be the potential of a cell in which the electroactive species are at unit activity in both compartments.

Thermodynamics of Galvanic Cells

The free energy change for a process represents the maximum amount of non-*PV* work that can be extracted from it. In the case of an electrochemical cell, this work is due to the flow of electrons through the potential difference between the two electrodes. Note, however, that as the rate of electron flow (i.e., the current) increases, the potential difference must decrease; if we short-circuit the cell by connecting the two electrodes with a conductor having negligible resistance, the potential difference is zero and no work will be done. The full amount of work can be realized only if the cell operates at an infinitessimal rate- that is, *reversibly*.

The total amount of energy a reaction can supply under standard conditions at constant pressure and temperature is given by DH^o. If the reaction takes place by combining the reactants directly (no cell) or in a short-circuited cell, no work is done and the heat released is D*H*. If the reaction takes place in a cell that performs electrical work, then the heat released is diminished by the amount of electrical work done. In the limit of reversible operation, the heat released becomes D*H* = D*G*° + *T* D*S*.

Analytical applications of the Nernst Equation

A very large part of Chemistry is concerned, either directly or indirectly, with determining the concentrations of ions in solution. Any method that can accomplish such measurements using relatively simple physical techniques is bound to be widely exploited. Cell potentials are fairly easy to measure, and although the Nernst equation relates them to ionic activities rather than to concentrations, the difference between them becomes negligible in solutions where the total ionic concentration is less than about 10-3 M.

Determination of Solubility Products

The concentrations of ions in equilibrium with a sparingly soluble salt are sufficiently low that the Nernst equation can be used with little error. Rather than measuring the concentration of the relevant ions directly, the more common procedure is to set up a cell in which one of the electrodes involves the insoluble salt, and whose net cell reaction is just the dissolution of the salt.

The standard potential for the net reaction refers to a hypothetical solution in which the activities of the two ions are unity. The cell potential we actually observe corresponds to *E* in the Nernst equation, which is then solved for *Q* which gives *Ksp* directly.

Potentiometric Titrations

In many situations, accurate determination of an ion concentration by direct measurement of a cell potential is impossible due to the presence of other ions and a lack of information about activity coefficients. In such cases it is often possible to determine the ion indirectly by titration with some other ion. For example, the initial concentration of an ion such as Fe^{2+} can be found by titrating with a strong oxidizing agent such as Ce^{4+}. The titration is carried out in one side of a cell whose other half is a reference electrode:

Pt(*s*) | Fe^{2+}, Fe^{3+} | | *reference electrode*

Initially the left cell contains only Fe^{2+}. As the titrant is added, the ferrous ion is oxidized to Fe^{3+} in a reaction that is virtually complete:

$Fe^{2+} + Ce^{4}+ \rightarrow Fe^{3+} + Ce^{3+}$

The cell potential is followed as the Fe^{2+} is added in small increments. Once the first drop of titrant has been added, the potential of the left cell is controlled by the ratio of oxidized and reduced iron according to the Nernst equation.

$$E = 0.680 - 059\log \frac{\left[Fe^{3+}\right]}{\left[Fe^{2+}\right]}$$

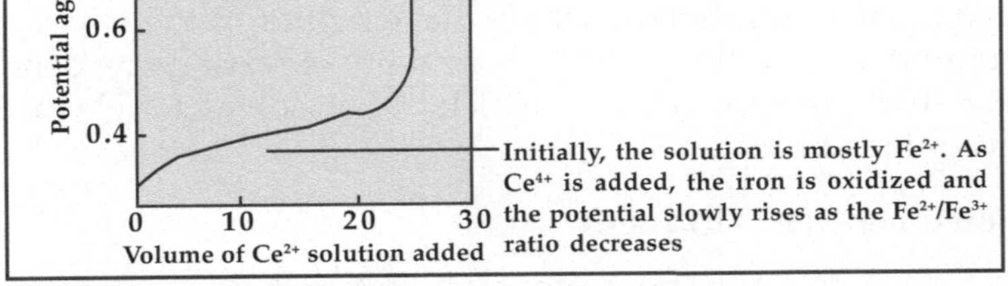

Fig. 3.13: **Potentiometric titration**

Plot showing how the cell potential changes when $FeSO_4$ is titrated with $Ce(SO_4)^2$. Note that the potential is controlled by different reactions on either side of the equivalance point.

When the equivalence point is reached, the Fe^{2+} will have been totally consumed (the large equilibrium constant ensures that this will be so), and the potential will then be controlled by the concentration ratio of Ce^{3+}/Ce^{4+}. The idea is that *both* species of a redox couple must be present in reasonable concentrations for a concentration to control the potential of an electrode of this kind. If one works out the actual cell potentials for various concentrations of all these species, the resulting titration curve looks much like the familiar acid-base titration curve. The end point is found not by measuring a particular cell voltage, but by finding what volume of titrant gives the steepest part of the curve.

Measurement of pH

Since pH is actually defined in terms of hydrogen ion *activity* and not its concentration, a hydrogen electrode allows a direct measure of $\{H^+\}$ and thus of $-\log \{H^+\}$, which is the pH.

Although this arrangement (in which the reference electrode could be a standard hydrogen electrode) has been used for high-precision determinations, it would be impractical for routine pH measurements of the kinds that are widely done, especially outside the laboratory.

The Glass Electrode for pH Measurements

In 1914 it was discovered that a thin glass membrane enclosing a solution of HCl can produce a potential that varies with $\{H^+\}$ in about the same way as that of the hydrogen electrode. Glass electrodes are manufactured in huge numbers for both laboratory and field measurements. They contain a built-in Ag-AgCl reference electrode in contact with the HCl solution enclosed by the membrane.

The potential of a glass electrode is given by a form of the Nernst equation very similar to that of an ordinary hydrogen electrode, but of course without the H^2:

$$E_{\text{membrane}} = \text{constant} + \frac{RT}{F}\ln\left([H^{+}] + \text{constant}\right)$$

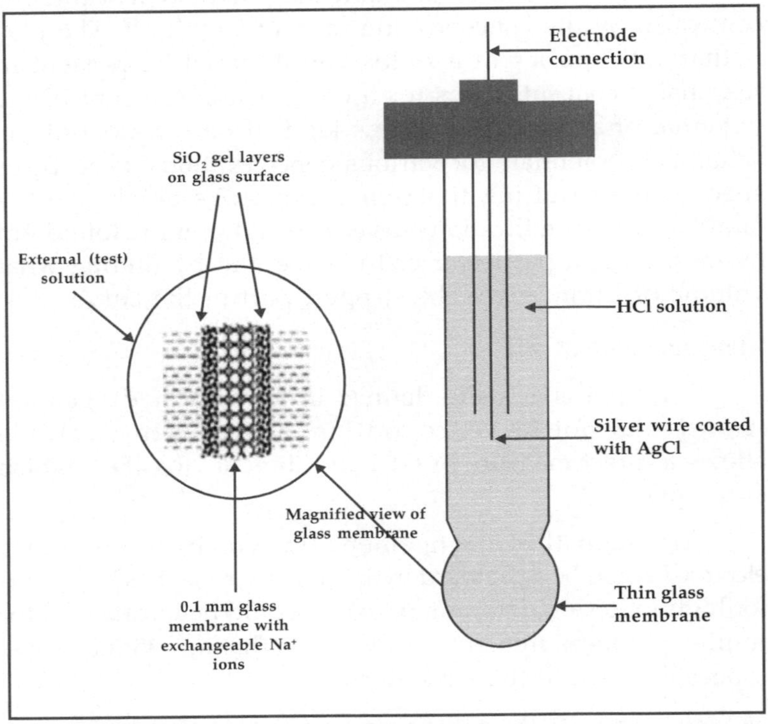

Fig. 3.14: **The glass electrode for pH measurements**

The reason a glass membrane would behave in this way was not understood until around 1970. It now appears that hydrogen ions in the external solution diffuse through the glass and push out a corresponding number of the Na+ ions which are normally present in most glasses. These sodium ions diffuse to whichever side of the membrane has the lower concentration, where they remain mostly confined to the surface of the glass, which has a porous, gelatinous nature. It is the excess charge produced by these positive ions that gives rise to the pH-dependent potential.

Ion-selective Electrodes

The function of the membrane in the glass electrode is to allow hydrogen ions to pass through and thus change its potential, while preventing other cations from doing the same thing (this selectivity is never perfect; most glass electrodes will respond to moderate concentrations of sodium ions, and to high concentrations of some others.) A glass electrode is thus one form of *ion-selective electrode*. Since about 1970, various other membranes have been developed which show similar selectivities to certain other ions. These are widely used in industrial, biochemical, and environmental applications.

Membrane Potentials

You may recall the phenomena of osmosis and osmotic pressure that are observed when two solutions having different solute concentrations are separated by a thin film or membrane whose porosity allows small ions and molecules to diffuse through, but which holds back larger particles.

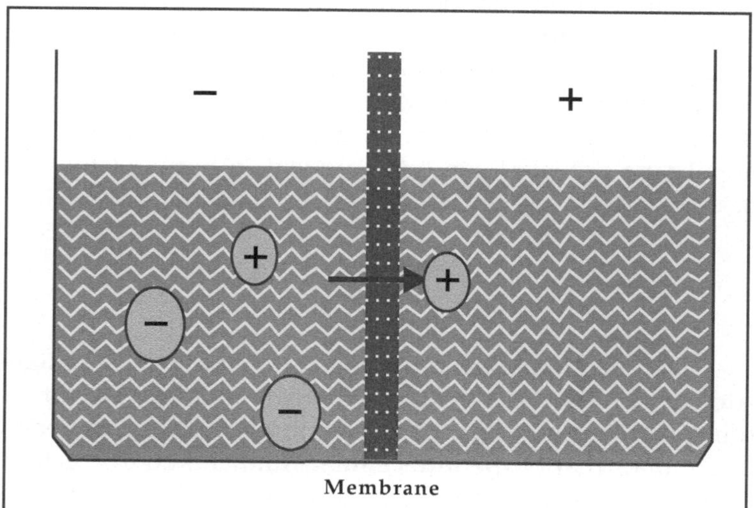

Fig. 3.15: **Origin of a membrane potential**

If one solution contains a pair of oppositely-charged ionic species whose sizes are very different, the smaller ions may pass through the semipermeable membrane while the larger ones are retained. This will produce a charge imbalance between the two solutions, with the original solution having the charge sign of the larger ion. Eventually the electrical work required to bring about further separation of charges becomes too large to allow any further net diffusion to take place, and the system settles into an equilibrium state in which a constant potential difference (usually around a volt or less) is maintained. This potential difference is usually called a *membrane potential* or *Donnan potential*.

If the smaller ions are able to diffuse through the membrane but the larger ions cannot, a potential difference will develop between the two solutions. This membrane potential can be observed by introducing a pair of platinum electrodes.

The figure shows a simple system containing the potassium salt of a protein on one side of a membrane, and potassium chloride on the other. The proteinate anion, being too large to diffuse through the membrane, gives rise to the potential difference. The value of this potential difference can be expressed by a relation that is essentially the same as the Nernst equation, although its derivation is different. The membrane potential can be expressed in terms of the ratio of either the K^+ or Cl^- ion activities:

$$\Delta\Phi = \frac{RT}{nF}\ln\frac{\{K\}_{right}}{\{K^+\}_{left}} = \frac{RT}{nF}\ln\frac{\{Cl^-\}_{left}}{\{Cl^-\}_{right}}$$

The membrane surrounding most living cells contains sites or "channels" through which K^+ ions are selectively transported so that the concentration of K^+ inside the cell is 10-30 times that of the intracellular fluid. Taking the activity ratio as about 20, the above equation predicts that the potential difference q*inside* – q*inside* will be

$$\Delta\Phi = 0.059\log\left(\frac{1}{20}\right) = -70\text{mv}$$

which is consistent with observed values. Transport of an ion such as K^+ from a region of low concentration into the more concentrated intercellular fluid requires a source of free energy, which is supplied by ATP under enzymatic control. The metabolic processes governing this action are often referred to as "ion pumps".

Nerve Conduction

Transmission of signals through the nervous system occurs not by the movement of a charge carrier through the nerve, but by waves of differential ion concentrations that travel along the length of the nerve. These concentration gradients are reduced by protein-based *ion channels* and ATP-activated (and energy-consuming) *ion pumps* specific to K^+ and Ca^{2+} ions.

4

Batteries and Fuel Cells

One of the oldest and most important applications of electrochemistry is to the storage and conversion of energy. You already know that a *galvanic cell* converts chemical energy to work; similarly, an *electrolytic cell* converts electrical work into chemical *free energy*. Devices that carry out these conversions are called *batteries*. In ordinary batteries the chemical components are contained within the device itself. If the reactants are supplied from an external source as they are consumed, the device is called a *fuel cell*.

The term *battery* derives from the older use of this word to describe physical attack or "beating"; Benjamin Franklin first applied the term to the electrical shocks that could be produced by an array of charged glass plates. In common usage, the term "call" is often used in place of battery.

The Ideal and the Real

For portable and transportation applications especially, a battery or fuel cell should store (and be able to deliver) the maximum amount of energy at the desired rate (power level) from a device that has the smallest possible weight and volume. The following parameters are commonly used to express these attributes:

- Storage capacity or *charge density*, coulombs/liter or coulombs/kg;
- *Energy density*, J/kg or watt-hour/lb
- *Power density*, watts/kg
- *Voltage efficiency*, ratio of output voltage to E°
- Lifetime: *shelf-life* (resistance to self-discharge) or *charge/recharge cycles*

Physical Limitations of Battery Performance

The most important of these are:

- *Effective surface area of the electrode*. A 1-cm2 sheet of polished metal presents far less active surface than does one that contains numerous surface projections or pores. All useful batteries and fuel cells employ highly porous electrodes.
- *Current density of electrode surface*. Expressed in amperes m–2, this is essentially a measure of the catalytic ability of the electrode, that is, its ability to reduce the activation energy of the electron transfer process.
- *Rate at which electroactive components can be delivered to or depart from the active electrode surface*. These processes are controlled by thermal diffusion and are inhibited by the very narrow pores that are needed to produce the large active surface area.
- *Side reactions and irreversible processes*. The products of the discharge reaction may tend to react with the charge-storing components. Thermal diffusion can also cause self-discharge, limiting the shelf life of the battery. Recharging of some storage batteries may lead to formation of less active modifications of solid phases, thus reducing the number of charge/discharge cycles possible. Clearly, these are all primarily kinetic and mechanistic factors which require a great deal of experimentation to understand and optimize.

Primary and Secondary Batteries

The electrode reactions in a *secondary* or *storage* battery can proceed in either direction, so the battery is capable of being recharged. During charging, electrical work is done on the cell to provide the free energy needed to force the reaction in its non-spontaneous direction. A *primary cell*, as expemplified by an ordinary flashlight battery, cannot be recharged with any efficiency, so the amount of energy it can deliver is limited to that obtainable from the reactants that were placed in it at the time of manufacture.

The Lead-acid Storage Cell

The most well-known storage cell is the lead-acid cell, which was invented by Gaston Planté 1859 and is still the most widely used device of its type.

The cell is represented by

$$Pb(s) \mid PbSO_4(s) \mid H_2SO_4(aq) \mid\mid PbSO_4(s), PbO_2(s) \mid Pb(s)$$

and the net cell reaction is

$$Pb(s) + PbO_2(s) + 2\,H_2SO_4(aq) \rightarrow 2\,PbSO_4(s) + 2\,H_2O$$

The reaction proceeds to the right during discharge and to the left during charging. The state of charge can be estimated by measuring the density of the electrolyte; sulfuric acid is about twice as dense as water, so as the cell is discharged, the density of the electrolyte decreases.

The technology of lead-acid storage batteries has undergone remarkably little change since the late 19th century. Their main drawback as power sources for electric vehicles is the weight of the lead; the maximum energy density is only about 35 Ah/kg, and actual values may be only half as much. There are also a few other problems:

- The sulfuric acid electrolyte becomes quite viscous when the temperature is low, inhibiting the flow of ions between the plated and reducing the current that can be delivered. The effect is well-known to anyone who has had difficulty starting a car in cold weather.

- These batteries tend to slowly self-discharge, so a car left idle for several weeks might be unable to start.
- Over time, PbSO4 that does not get converted to PbO_2 due to lack of complete discharge gradually changes to an inert form which limits the battery capacity. Also, "fast" charging causes rapid evolution of hydrogen from the water in the electrolyte; the bubbles form on the lead surface and can tear PbO2 off the positive plate. Eventually enough solid material accumulates at the bottom of the electrolyte to short-circuit the battery, leading to its permanent demise.

The LeClanché "dry cell"

The most well-known primary battery has long been the common "dry cell" that is widely used to power flashlights and similar devices. The modern dry cell is based on the on invented by *Georges Leclanché* in 1866. The electrode reactions are:

$$Zn \rightarrow Zn^{2+} + 2e-$$

$$2\ MnO_2 + 2H+ + 2e^- \rightarrow Mn_2O_3 + H_2O$$

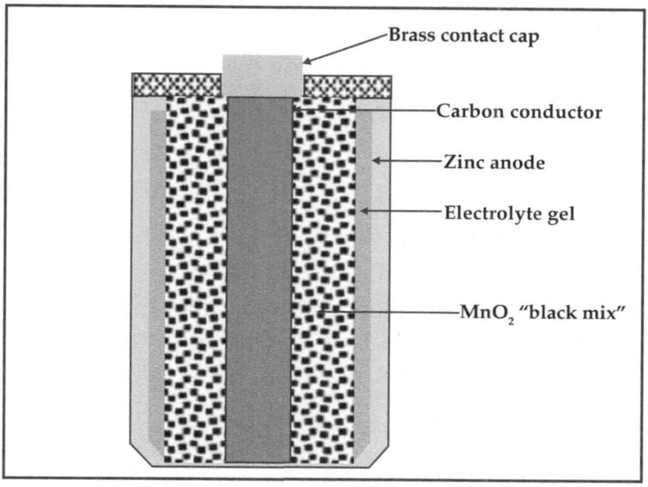

Fig. 4.1: **A Modern Leclanche cell**

Despite its name, this cell is not really "dry"; the electrolyte is a wet paste containing NH_4Cl to supply the hydrogen ions. The chemistry of this cell is more complicated than it would appear from these equations, and there are many side reactions. A more modern version, introduced in 1949, is the *alkaline cell* hich employs a KOH electrolyte and a zinc-powder anode which permits the cell to deliver higher currents.

The Fuel Cell

Conventional batteries supply electrical energy from the chemical reactants stored within them; when these reactants are consumed, the battery is "dead". An alternative approach would be to feed the reactants into the cell as they are required, so as to permit the cell to operate continuously. In this case the reactants can be thought of as "fuel" to drive the cell, hence the term fuel cell. Although fuel cells were not employed for practical purposes until space exploration began in the 1960's, the principle was first demonstrated in 1839 by Sir William Grove, a lawyer and amateur chemist. At the time, it was already known that water could be decomposed into hydrogen and oxygen by electrolysis; Grove tried recombining the two gases in a simple apparatus, and discovered what he called "reverse electrolysis":

anode: $H2(g) \rightarrow 2H^+ + 2e^-$ $\quad E^\circ = 0$ v

cathode: $\frac{1}{2} O_2 + 2H^+ + 2e^- \rightarrow H_2O(l)$ $\quad E^\circ = 1.23\ v$

net: $H_2(g) + \frac{1}{2} O_2\ (g) \rightarrow H_2O(l)$ $\quad E^\circ = +1.23\ v$

It was not until 1959 that the first working hydrogen-oxygen fuel cell was developed. Modern cells employ an lkaline electrolyte, so the electrode reactions differ from the ne shown above by the addition of OH^- to both sides of the equations (note that the net reaction is the same):

anode: $H_2(g) + 2\ OH^- \rightarrow 2\ H_2O + 2\ e^-$ $\quad E^\circ = ov$

cathode: $\frac{1}{2} O_2\ (g) + 2\ H_2O + 2\ e^- \rightarrow 2\ OH^-$ $\quad E^\circ = +1.23v$

net: $H_2(g) + \frac{1}{2} O_2(g) \rightarrow H_2O$ $\quad E^\circ = +1.23v$

In place of dihydrogen, other fuels such as alcohols, ydrocarbon liquids, and even coal slurries have been used; methanol appears to be an especially promising fuel.

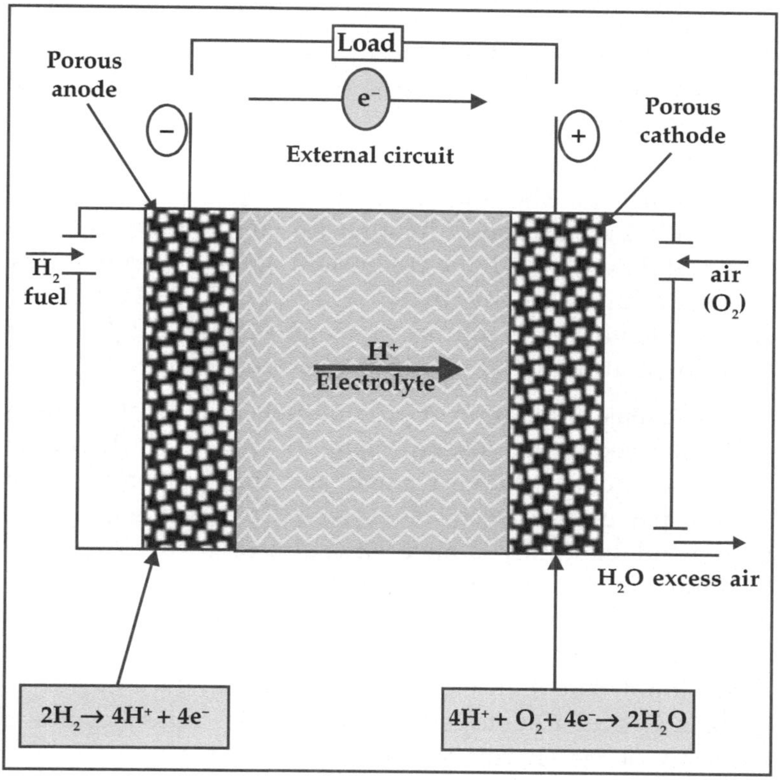

Fig. 4.2: **Diagram of modern hydrogen oxygen fuel cell**

In a fuel cell, the oxidation and reduction steps take place in separate compartments, unlike in conventional combustion. The fuel in this particular cell is hydrogen, but methanol or any other fuel can also be used. Developing suitably active and permanent catalytic electrode surfaces is the principal engineering problem.

One reason for the interest in fuel cells is that they offer a far more efficient way of utilizing chemical energy than does conventional thermal conversion. The work obtainable in the limit of reversible operation of a fuel cell is 229 kJ per mole of H_2O formed. If the hydrogen were simply burned in oxygen, the heat obtainable would be $-\Delta H^\circ = 242$ kJ mol^{-1}, but no more than about half of this heat can be converted into work so the output would not exceed 121 kJ mol^{-1}.

This limit is a consequence of the *Second Law of Thermodynamics*. The fraction of heat that can be converted into work is a function of how far (in temperature) the heat falls as it flows through the engine and into the surroundings; this fraction is given by $(1 - T_{high})/ T_{low}$. At normal environmental temperatures of around 300K, Thigh would have to be at least 600 forK 50% thermal efficiency.

The major limitation of present fuel cells is that the rates of the electrode reactions, especially the one in which oxygen is reduced, tend to be very small, and thus so is the output current per unit of electrode surface. Coating the electrode with a suitable catalytic material is almost always necessary to obtain usable output currents, but good catalysts are mostly very expensive substances such as platinum, so that the resulting cells are too costly for most practical uses. There is no doubt that if an efficient, low-cost catalytic electrode surface is ever developed, the fuel cell would become a mainstay of the energy economy.

Electrochemical Corrosion

Corrosion can be defined as the deterioration of materials by chemical processes. Of these, the most important by far is electrochemical corrosion of metals, in which the oxidation process

$M \rightarrow M+ {}^{+} e-$ is facilitated by the presence of a suitable electron acceptor, sometimes referred to in corrosion science as a *depolarizer*.

In a sense, corrosion can be viewed as the spontaneous return of metals to their ores; the huge quantities of energy that were consumed in mining, refining, and manufacturing metals into useful objects is dissipated by a variety of different routes.

The economic aspects of corrosion are far greater than most people realize; according to a report published in 2001, the cost of corrosion in the U.S. alone was $276 billion per year. Of this, about $121 billion was spent to control corrosion, leaving the difference of $155 billion as the net loss to the economy. Utilities, especially drinking water and sewer systems, suffer the largest economic impactwith motor vehicles and transportation being a close second. Corrosion is the destructive attack of a metal by chemical or electrochemical reaction with its environment. Under normal environmental con itions, the thermodynamically stable states of most of the metallic elements are the cations, rather han the metal itself. This is the reason that considerable energy (and expense) must go into the extraction of a metal from its ore. However, once the metal is won and put into use, it tends to spontaneously revert back to its more stable form. To do so, the metal must lose electrons, and this requires the presence of an electron acceptor or oxidizing agent. Oxygen, of course, is he most prominent of these, but hydrogen ions and the cations of any more "noble" metall are also very common promoters of corrosion. The special characteristic of most corrosion processes is that the oxidation and reduction steps occur at separate ocations on the metal. This is possible because metals are conductive, so the electrons can flow through the metal from the anodic to the cathodic regions. In this sense the system can be regarded as an electrochemical cell in which the anodic process is something like

$$Fe(s) \rightarrow Fe^{2+}(aq) + 2\,e^-$$

and the cathodic steps can be any of

$$O_2 + 2\,H_2O + 4e^- \rightarrow 4\,OH^-$$

$$H^+ + e^- \rightarrow \tfrac{1}{2}\,H_2(g)$$

$$M^{2+} + 2\,e^- \rightarrow M(s)$$

where M is a metal. A thin film of moisture on the surface of the metal can serve as the medium for the electrolyte. Which parts of the metal serve as anodes and cathodes can depend on many factors, as can be seen from the irregular corrosion patterns that are commonly observed. Atoms in regions that have undergone stress, as might be produced by forming or machining, often tend to have higher free energies, and thus tend to become anodic.

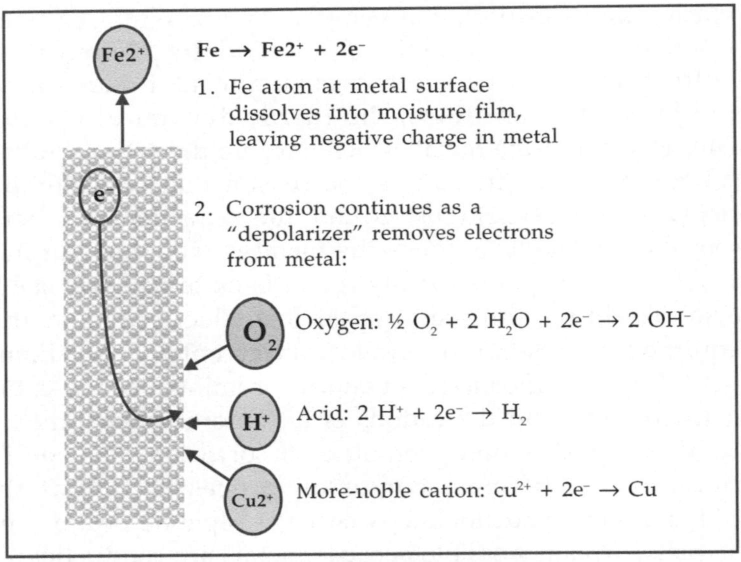

Fig. 4.3: **Electrochemical corrosion of iron**

Corrosion often begins at a location where the metal is stressed in some way or isolated from oxygen, such as between joints or under a paint film. The metal ions dissolve in the moisture film and the electrons migrate to another location where they are taken up by a "depolarizer". Oxygen is the most common depolarizer; the resulting hydroxide ions react with the Fe^{2+} to form the mixture of hydrous iron oxides known as "rust".

For part of a metal to act as the site for oxidation and dissolution, it must be in contact with 1. A noble metal is one that appears toward the bottom of a listing of standard reduction serve as lower-free energy sinks which can accept electrons from higher (less noble) metals.

The electrolyte, which may be no more than a film of adsorbed moisture. However, practically all metallic surfaces that have been exposed to the atmosphere are coated with a thin film of the metal oxide, which tends to shield the metal from the electrolyte and thus prevent corrosion.

If one part of a metallic object is protected from the atmosphere so that there is insufficient O_2 to build or maintain the oxide film, this "protected" region will often be the site at which corrosion is most active. The fact that such sites are usually hidden from view accounts for much of the difficulty in detecting and controlling corrosion.

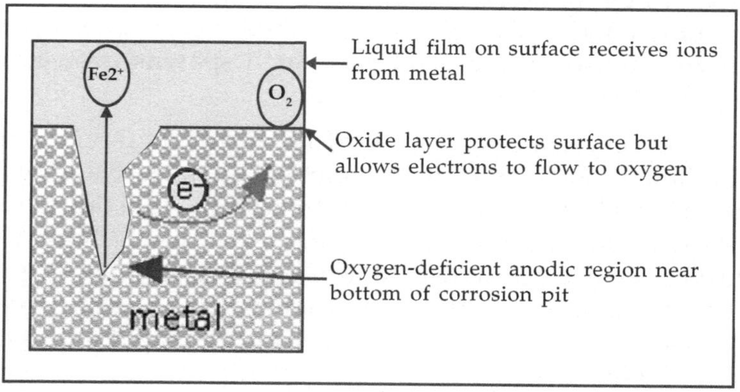

Fig. 4.4: **Pitting corrosion**

Most metals are covered with thin layer of oxide film which inhibits anodic dissolution. When corrosion does occur, it sometimes hollows out a narrow hole, or pit, in the metal. The bottoms of these pits tend to be deprived of oxygen, thus promoting further growth of the pit into the metal. Many oxides have semiconductive properties and thus do not interfere with the flow of electrons to O_2.

In contrast to anodic sites, which tend to be localized to specific regions of the surface, the cathodic part of the process can occur almost anywhere. Because metallic oxides are usually semiconductors, most oxide coatings do not inhibit the flow of electrons to the surface, so almost any region that is exposed to O_2 or to some other electron acceptor can act as a cathode. The tendency of oxygen-deprived locations to become anodic is the cause of many commonlyobserved patterns of corrosion. Rusted-out cars and bathroom stains. Anyone who has owned an older car has seen corrosion occur at joints between body parts and under paint films. You will also have noticed that once corrosion starts, it tends to feed on itself. One reason for this is that one of the products of the O_2 reduction reaction is hydroxide ion. The high pH produced in these cathodic regions tends to destroy the protective oxide film, and may even soften or weaken paint films, so that these sites can become anodic. The greater supply of electrons promotes more intense cathodic action, which spawns even more anodic sites, and so on.

A very common cause of corrosion is having two dissimilar metals in contact, as might occur near a fastener or at a weld joint. Moisture collects at the junction point, acting as an electrolyteand forming a cell in which the two metals serve as electrodes. Moisture and conductive salts on the outside surfaces acts as an external conductor, effectively short-circuiting he cell and producing very rapid corrosion; this is why cars rust out so quickly in places where salt is placed on roads to melt ice.

Dissimilar-metal corrosion can occur even if the two metals are not initially in direct contact. For example, in homes where copper tubing is used for plumbing, there is always a small amount of dissolved Cu^{2+} in the water. When this water encounters steel piping or a chromeplated bathroom sink drain, the more-noble copper will plate out on the other metal, producing a new metals-in-contact corrosion cell. In the case of chrome bathroom sink fittings, this leads to the formation of Cr^{3+} salts which precipitate as greenish stains.

Metals such as aluminum and stainless steels form extremely tough and adherent oxide films that afford extraordinary corrosion resistance.

Control of Corrosion

Since both the cathodic and anodic steps must take place for corrosion to occur, prevention of either one will stop corrosion. The most obvious strategy is to stop both processes by coating the object with a paint or other protective coating. Even if this is done, there are likely to be places where the coating is broken or does not penetrate, particularly if there are holes or screw threads. A more sophisticated approach is to apply a slight negative charge to the metal, thus making it more difficult for the reaction $M \rightarrow M^{2+} + 2\,e^-$ to take place.

Sacrificial Coatings

One way of supplying this negative charge is to apply a coating of a more active metal. Thus a very common way of protecting steel from corrosion is to coat it with a thin layer of zinc; this process is known as *galvanizing*. The zinc coating, being less noble than iron, tends to corrode selectively. Dissolution of this *sacrificial coating* leaves behind electrons which concentrate in the iron, making it cathodic and thus inhibiting its dissolution.

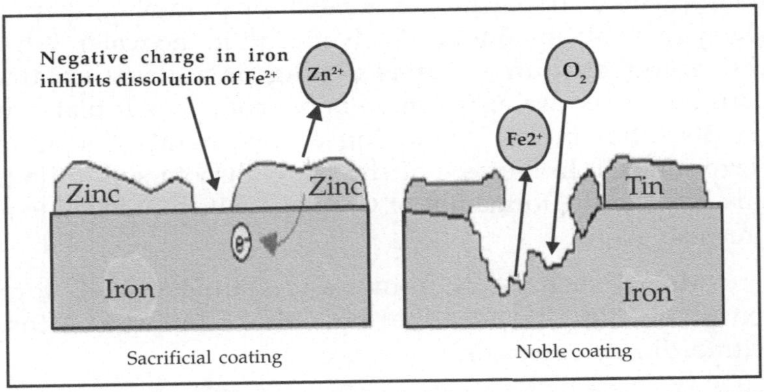

Fig. 4.5: **Corrosion protection by sacrificial coating, and its reverse**

The effect of plating iron with a less active metal provides an interesting contrast. The common tin-plated can (on the right of Fig. 4.5) is a good example. As long as the tin coating remains intact, all is well, but exposure of even a tiny part of the underlying iron to the moist atmosphere initiates corrosion. The electrons released from the iron flow into the tin, making the iron more anodic so now the tin is actively promoting corrosion of the iron! You have probably observed how tin cans disintegrate very rapidly when left outdoors.

Cathodic Protection

Another way of keeping metal in a cathodic state is to connect it to an external direct current source. For smaller structures such as boats and domestic water water heaters the current is supplied by a sacrificial anode made of aluminum or zinc. For larger extended structures such as piers and buried pipelines, an external line-operated or photovoltaic power supply is commonly used.

5

Electrolytic Cells

Electrolysis refers to the decomposition of a substance by an electric current. The electrolysis of sodium and potassium hydroxides, first carried out in 1808 by Sir Humphrey Davey, led to the discovery of these two metallic elements and showed that these two hydroxides which had previously been considered undecomposable and thus elements, were in fact compounds.

"By means of a flame which was thrown on a spoon containing potash, this alkali was kept for some minutes at a strong red heat, and in a state of perfect fluidity."

One pole of a battery of copper-zinc cells was connected to the spoon, and the other was connected to platinum wire which dipped into the melt. "By this arrangement some brilliant phenomena were produced. The potash appeared to be a conductor in a high degree, and as long as the communication was preserved, a most intense light was exhibited at the negative wire, and a column of flame, which seemed to be owing to the development of combustible matter, arose from the point of contact." The flame was due to the combustion in the air of metallic potassium. In another experiment, Davey observed "small globules having a high metallic lustre, precisely similar in visible characters to quicksilver, some of which burnt with explosion and bright flame, as soon as they were formed, and others remained, and were merely tarnished, and finally covered by a white film which formed on their surfaces."

Electrolysis of molten alkali halides is the usual industrial method of preparing the alkali metals:

Cathode reaction: $Na^+ + e^- \rightarrow Na(l)$ E° = –2.71 V

Anode reaction: $Cl^- \rightarrow \frac{1}{2} Cl_2(g) + e-$ E° = –1.36 V

Net reaction: $Na^+ + Cl^- \rightarrow Na(l) + \frac{1}{2} Cl_2(g)$ E° = –4.1 V

Ions in aqueous solutions can undergo similar reactions. Thus if a solution of nickel chloride undergoes electrolysis at platinum electrodes, the reactions are:

Cathode reaction: Ni^{2+} + 2 e– → Ni(s) E° = –0.24 V

Anode reaction: 2 Cl– → Cl2(*g*) + 2 e– E° = –1.36 v

Net reaction: $Ni^{2+} + 2 Cl^- \rightarrow Ni(s) + Cl_2(g)$ E° = – 1.60 v

Both of these processes are carried out in electrochemical cells which are forced to operate in the "reverse", or non-spontaneous direction, as indicated by the negative for the above cell reaction. The free energy is supplied in the form of electrical work done on the system by the outside world (the surroundings). This is the only fundamental difference between an *electrolytic* cell and the *galvanic* cell in which the free energy supplied by the cell reaction is extracted as work done on the surroundings.

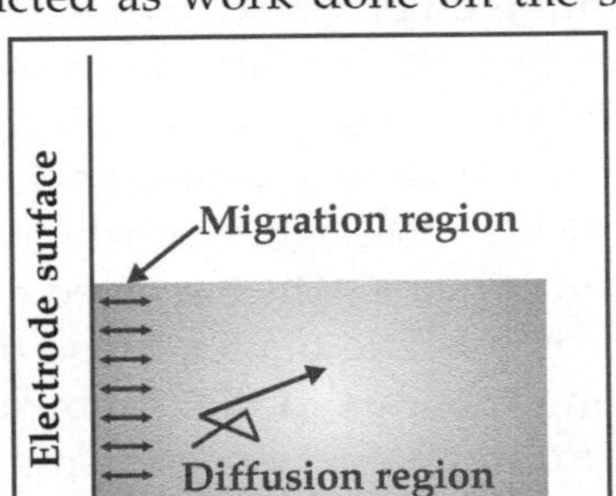

***Fig. 5.1*: Diffusion and migration in an electrolytic cell**

A common misconception about electrolysis is that "ions are attracted to the oppositely-charged electrode." This is true only in the very thin interfacial region near the electrode surface.

Ionic motion throughout the bulk of the solution is by *diffusion*, which is the transport of molecules in response to a concentration gradient. *Migration*—the motion of a charged particle due to an applied electric field, is only a minor player, producing only about one non-random jump out of around 100,000 random ones for a 1 volt cm–1 electric field. Only those ion that find themselves within the interfacial region are likely to undergo migration.

Electrolysis in Aqueous Solutions

Water is capable of undergoing both

oxidation $H_2O \rightarrow O_2(g) + 4\ H^+ + 2\ e^-$ $E^o = -1.23\ v$

and

reduction $2\ H_2O + 2\ e^- \rightarrow H_2(g) + 2\ OH^-$ $E^o = -0.83\ v$

Thus if an aqueous solution is subjected to electrolysis, one or both of the above reactions may be able to compete with the electrolysis of the solute. This does not happen for the solution of $NiCl_2$ illustrated above, but if we substitute sodium chloride for nickel chloride, hydrogen is produced at the cathode instead of sodium:

cathode: $H_2O + 2\ e^- \rightarrow H_2(g) + 2$ OH– $E =$
$+0.41\ v$ ([OH–] = 10–7 *M*)

anode: $Cl^- \rightarrow \frac{1}{2}\ Cl_2(g) +$ e– $E^o = -1.36\ v$

net: $Cl^- + H_2O \rightarrow 2\ H_2(g) + \frac{1}{2}\ Cl_2(g) + 2\ OH^-$

The reason metallic sodium is not a product of this reaction is best understood by locating the couples

Na/Na^+ and H_2O/H_2, OH^- Na^+ (E^o = –2.7 v) is energetically more difficult than the reduction of water, so in aqueous solution the latter will prevail. If we replace the chloride ion in the above reaction with an anion such as nitrate or sulfate that is energetically much more difficult to oxidize, the water is oxidized instead. Electrolysis of a solution of sulfuric acid or of a salt such as $NaNO_3$ results in the decomposition of water at both electrodes:

cathode: $H_2O + 2e^- \rightarrow H_2(g) + 2 OH^-$ *E* =+0.41 *v* ([OH–] = 10–7 *M*)

anode: $2 H_2O \rightarrow O_2(g) + 4 H^+ + 2 e-$ $E^o = -0.82$ v

net: $2 H_2O(l) \rightarrow 2 H_2(g) + O_2(g)$ $E = -1.23$ v

Faraday's Laws of Electrolysis

One mole of electric charge (96,500 coulombs), when passed through a cell, will discharge half a mole of a divalent metal ion such as $Cu2^+$. This relation was first formulated by Faraday in 1832 in the form of two *laws of electrolysis*:

1. The weights of substances formed at an electrode during electrolysis are directly proportional to the quantity of electricity that passes through the electrolyte.
2. The weights of different substances formed by the passage of the same quantity of electricity are proportional to the equivalent weight of each substance.

The *equivalent weight* of a substance is defined as the molar mass, divided by the number of electrons required to oxidize or reduce each unit of the substance. Thus one mole of V3+ corresponds to three equivalents of this species, and will require three faradays of charge to deposit it as metallic vanadium.

Most stoichiometric problems involving electrolysis can be solved without explicit use of Faraday's laws. The "chemistry" in these problems is usually very elementary; the major difficulties usually stem from unfamiliarity with the basic electrical units:

- *current* (amperes) is the rate of *charge transport*; 1 amp = 1 c/sec.

- *power* (watts) is the rate of *energy* production or consumption; 1_w = 1 J/sec = 1 volt-amp; 1 watt-sec = 1 J, 1 k_w-h = 3600 J.

Example

Metallic object to be plated with copper is placed in a solution of $CuSO_4$ which electrode of a direct current power supply should the object be connected?

What mass of copper will be deposited if a current of 0.22 amp flows through the cell for 1.5 hours? Since $Cu2^+$ ions are being reduced, the object acts as a cathode and must be connected to the negative terminal (where the electrons come from!)

The amount of charge passing through the cell is (0.11 amp) × (54600 sec) = 1200 c (1200 c) ÷ (96500 c F–1) = 0.124 F

Since the reduction of one mole of $Cu2^+$ ion requires the addition of two moles of electrons, 0.124 F will discharge only 0.062 mol of $Cu2^+$ whose mass will be (0.062 mol) × (63.54 g mol–1) = 3.94 g of copper.

Industrial Electrolytic Processes

For many industrial-scale operations involving the oxidation or reduction of both inorganic nd organic substances, and especially for the production of the more active metals such as sodium, calcium, magnesium, and aluminum, the most cost-effective reducing agent is electrons supplied by an external power source.

The Chloralkali Industry

The electrolysis of brine is carried out on a huge scale for the industrial production of chlorine and caustic soda (sodium hydroxide). Because the reduction potential of Na^+ is much higher than that of water, the latter substance undergoes decomposition at the cathode, yielding hydrogen gas and OH^-.

anode	$2\,Cl^- \rightarrow Cl_2\,(g) + 2\,e^-$	-1.36 v	*i*
reactions	$4\,OH^- \rightarrow O_2(g) + 2\,H_2O + 4\,e^-$	-0.40 v	*ii*
cathode	$Na^+ + e^- \rightarrow Na\,(s)$	-2.7 v	*iii*
reactions	$H_2O + 2\,e^- \rightarrow H_2(g) + 2\,OH^-$	+.41 v	*iv*

A comparison of the E^os would lead us to predict that the reduction (*ii*) would be favoured over that of (*i*). This is certainly the case from a purely energetic standpoint, but as was mentioned in the section on fuel cells, electrode reactions involving O_2 are notoriously slow (that is, they are *kinetically thin ered*), so the anodic process here is under kinetic rather than thermodynamic control. The reduction of water (*iv*) is energetically favoured over that of Na^+ (iii), so the net result of the electrolysis of brine is the production of Cl_2 and NaOH ("*caustic*"), both of which are of immense industrial importance:

$$2\,NaCl + 2\,H_2O \rightarrow 2\,NaOH + Cl_2(g) + H_2(g)$$

Since chlorine reacts with both OH^- and H_2, it is necessary to physically separate the anode and cathode compartments. In modern plants this is accomplished by means of an ion-selective polymer membrane, but prior to 1970 a more complicated cell was used that employed a pool of mercury as the cathode. A small amount of this mercury would normally find its way into the plant's waste stream, and this has resulted serious pollution of many major river systems and estuaries and devastation of their fisheries. Even though these mercury cells have now mostly been removed, the aquatic pollution will continue for hundreds of years as the mercury is slowly released from bottom sediments.

Electrolytic Refining of Aluminum

Aluminum is present in most rocks and is the most abundant metallic element in the earth's crust (eight per cent by weight.) However, its isolation is very difficult and expensive to accomplish by purely chemical means, as evidenced by the high E° (–1.66 v) of the Al^{3+}/Al couple. For the same reason, aluminum cannot be isolated by electrolysis of aqueous solutions of its compounds, since the water would be electrolyzed preferentially. And if you have ever tried to melt a rock, you will appreciate the difficulty of electrolyzing a molten aluminum ore! Aluminum was in fact considered an exotic and costly metal until 1886, when Charles Hall (U.S.A) and Paul Hérault (France) independently developed a practical electrolytic reduction process.

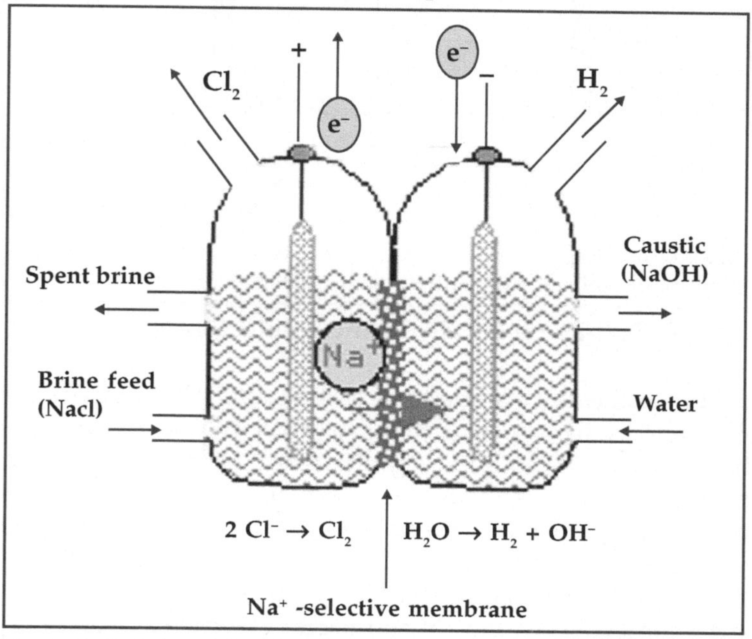

Fig. 5.2: **Schematic diagram of a modern cell for the production of chlorine**

The Hall-Hérault process takes advantage of the principle that the melting point of a substance is reduced by admixture with another substance with which it forms a homogeneous phase. Instead of using the pure alumina ore Al_2O_3 which melts at 2050°C, it is mixed with cryolite, which is a natural mixture of NaF and AlF_3, thus reducing the temperature required to a more manageable 1000°C. The

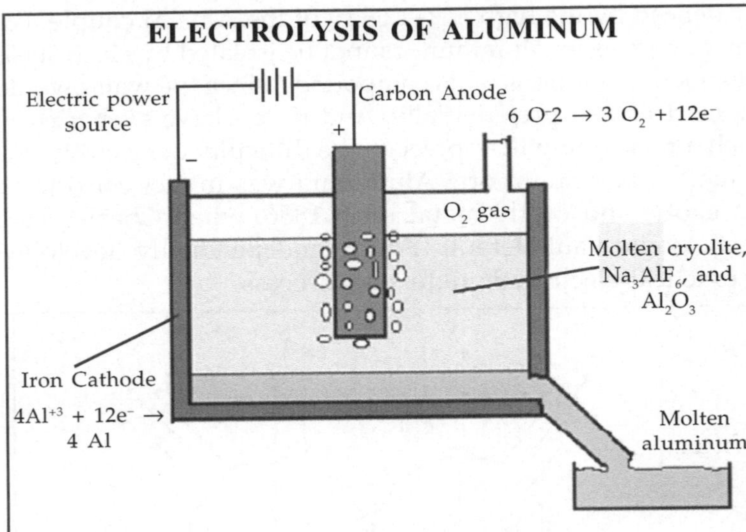

Bauxite ore is purified to Al_2O_3, which is mixed with cryolite, a mixture of NaF and AlF_3, which melts at 1000 C

Fig. 5.3: **Hall-Hérault cell for the production of aluminum**

anodes of the cell are made of carbon (actually a mixture of pitch and coal), and this plays a direct role in the process; the carbon gets oxidized (by the oxide ions left over from the reduction of Al^{3+}) to CO, and the free energy of this reaction helps drive the aluminum reduction, lowering the voltage that must be applied and thus reducing the power consumption. This is important, because aluminum refining is the largest consumer of industrial electricity, accounting for about 5% of all electricity generated in North America. Since aluminum cells commonly operate at about 100,000 amperes, even a slight reduction in voltage can result in a large saving of power. The net reaction is $2\ Al_2O_3 + 3\ C \rightarrow 4\ Al + 3\ CO_2$ However, large quantities of CO and of HF (from the cryolite), and hydrocarbons (from the electrodes) are formed in various side reactions, and these can be serious sources of environmental pollution.

6

Electrochemical Gradient

An electrochemical gradient is a spatial variation of both electrical potential and chemical concentration across a membrane. Both components are often due to ion gradients, particularly proton gradients, and the result can be a type of potential energy available for work in a cell. This can be calculated as a thermodynamic measure, termed electrochemical potential, that combines the concepts of energy stored in the form of chemical potential, which accounts for an ion's concentration gradient across a cellular membrane, and electrostatics, which accounts for an ion's tendency to move relative to the membrane potential.

Overview

Electrochemical potential is important in electroanalytical chemistry and industrial applications such as batteries and fuel cells. It represents one of the many interchangeable forms of potential energy through which energy may be conserved.

In biological processes, the direction an ion moves by diffusion or active transport across a membrane is determined by the electrochemical gradient. In mitochondria and chloroplasts, proton gradients are used to generate a chemiosmotic potential that is also known as a proton motive force. This potential energy is used for the synthesis of ATP by oxidative phosphorylation.

An electrochemical gradient has two components. First, the electrical component is caused by a charge difference across the lipid membrane. Second, a chemical component is caused by a differential concentration of ions across the membrane. The combination of these two factors determines the thermo-dynamically favourable direction for an ion's movement across a membrane.

An electrochemical gradient is analogous to the water pressure across a hydroelectric dam. Membrane transport proteins such as the sodium-potassium pump within the membrane are equivalent to turbines that convert the water's potential energy to other forms of physical or chemical energy, and the ions that pass through the membrane are equivalent to water that ends up at the bottom of the dam. Also, energy can be used to pump water up into the lake above the dam. In similar manner, chemical energy in cells can be used to create electrochemical gradients.

Chemistry

The term is typically applied in contexts wherein a chemical reaction is to take place, such as one involving the transfer of an electron at a battery electrode. In a battery, an electrochemical potential arising from the movement of ions balances the reaction energy of the electrodes. The maximum voltage that a battery reaction can produce is sometimes called the standard electrochemical potential of that reaction. In instances pertaining specifically to the movement of electrically charged solutes, the potential is often expressed in units of volts.

Biological Context

In biology, the term is sometimes used in the context of a chemical reaction, in particular to describe the energy source for the chemical synthesis of ATP. In more general terms, however, it is used to characterize the tendency of solutes to simply diffuse across a membrane, a process involving no chemical transformation.

Ion Gradients

With respect to a cell, organelle, or other subcellular compartment, the tendency of an electrically charged solute, such as a potassium ion, to move across the membrane is decided by the difference in its electrochemical potential on either side of the membrane, which arises from three factors:

- the difference in the concentration of the solute between the two sides of the membrane;
- the charge or "valence" of the solute molecule;
- the difference in voltage between the two sides of the membrane (i.e. the transmembrane potential).

A solute's electrochemical potential difference is zero at its "reversal potential", the transmembrane voltage at which the solute's net flow across the membrane is also zero. This potential is predicted, in theory, either by the Nernst equation (for systems of one permeant ion species) or by the Goldman-Hodgkin-Katz equation (for more than one permeant ion species). Electrochemical potential is measured in the laboratory and field using reference electrodes.

Transmembrane ATPases or transmembrane proteins with ATPase domains are often used for making and utilizing ion gradients. The enzyme Na^+/K^+ ATPase uses ATP to make a sodium ion gradient and a potassium ion gradient. The electrochemical potential is used as energy storage. Chemiosmotic coupling is one of several ways a thermodynamically unfavourable reaction can be driven by a thermodynamically favorable one. Cotransport of ions by symporters and antiporter carriers is commonly used to actively move ions across biological membranes.

Proton Gradients

The proton gradient can be used as intermediate energy storage for heat production and flagellar rotation. In addition, it is an interconvertible form of energy in active transport, electron potential generation, NADPH synthesis, and ATP synthesis/hydrolysis.

The electrochemical potential difference between the two sides of the membrane in mitochondria, chloroplasts, bacteria, and other membranous compartments that engage in active transport involving proton pumps, is at times called a chemiosmotic potential or proton motive force (see chemiosmosis). In this context, protons are often considered separately using units of either concentration or pH.

Proton Motive Force

Two protons are expelled at each coupling site, generating the proton motive force (PMF). ATP is made indirectly using the PMF as a source of energy. Each pair of protons yields one ATP.

Some archaea, the most notable ones being halobacteria, make proton gradients by pumping in protons from the environment with the help of the solar-driven enzyme bacteriorhodopsin, which is used here for driving the molecular motor enzyme ATP synthase to make the necessary conformational changes required to synthesize ATP.

Proton gradients are also made by bacteria by running ATP synthase in reverse, and are used to drive flagella.

The F_1F_O ATP synthase is a reversible enzyme. Large enough quantities of ATP cause it to create a transmembrane proton gradient. This is used by fermenting bacteria - which do not have an electron transport chain, and hydrolyze ATP to make a proton gradient - for flagella and the transportation of nutrients into the cell.

In respiring bacteria under physiological conditions, ATP synthase, in general, runs in the opposite direction, creating ATP while using the proton motive force created by the electron transport chain as a source of energy. The overall process of creating energy in this fashion is termed oxidative phosphorylation. The same process takes place in mitochondria, where ATP synthase is located in the inner mitochondrial membrane, so that F1 part sticks into the mitochondrial matrix where ATP synthesis takes place.

Membrane Potential

Membrane potential (or transmembrane potential), is the voltage difference (or electrical potential difference) between the interior and exterior of a cell. Because the fluid inside and outside a cell is highly conductive, whereas a cell's plasma membrane is highly resistive, the voltage change in moving from a point outside to a point inside occurs largely within the narrow width of the membrane itself. Therefore, it is common to speak of the membrane potential as the voltage across the membrane.

The plasma membrane surrounds the cell to provide a stable environment for biological processes. The membrane potential arises from the action of ion channels, ion pumps, and ion transporters embedded in the membrane which maintain different ion concentrations inside and outside the cell. The term "membrane potential" is sometimes used interchangeably with cell potential but is applicable to any lipid bilayer or membrane.

Three special cases of physiological membrane potential with underlying mechanisms and the concept of equilibrium or reversal potential, which constitute the subject of electrophysiology and cellular biophysics, are addressed in this article. The former are resting membrane potential, action potential, and graded (postsynaptic) membrane potentials. The membrane potential of most not-excitable cells is kept at relatively stable value of resting potential. In contrast, electrically excitable cells like neurons and myocytes can "fire" action potentials. Neurons are specialized to use changes in membrane potential for fast communication, with other neurons, muscles, and secretory cells. When cell membrane depolarizes from resting potential and produces action potential, it travels down the axon to the synapses: the magnitude of the axonal membrane potential varies dynamically along its length. On reaching a (chemical) synapse, a neurotransmitter is released causing a localized change in potential in the postsynaptic membrane of the target neuron by opening ion channels in its membrane. Importantly, every occasion of action potential firing results from spatial and temporal summation of often a very large number of minuscule graded postsynaptic responses of both positive (membrane depolarization) and negative (membrane hyperpolarization) polarities. Ultimately, such important aspects as value of resting potential, maximum amplitude and after-hyperpolarization phase of action potential can be easily understood utilizing the concept of equilibrium potential.

In the case of the resting membrane potential across an animal cell's plasma membrane, potassium (and sodium) gradients are established by the Na^+/K^+-ATPase (sodium-potassium pump) which transports 2 potassium ions inside and 3 sodium ions outside at the cost of 1 ATP molecule. In other cases, for example, a membrane potential may be established by acidification of the inside of a membranous compartment (such as the proton pump that generates membrane potential across synaptic vesicle membranes).

Reversal Potential

An equilibrium or reversal potential of an ion is the value of transmembrane voltage at which the electric force generated by diffusional movement of the ion down its concentration gradient becomes equal to the molecular force of that diffusion. This means that the transmembrane voltage exactly matches (resists) the force of diffusion of the ion (or vice versa), such that the net current of the ion across the membrane is zero and unchanging. The equilibrium potential of a particular ion is designated by the notation E_{ion}. The equilibrium potential for any ion can be calculated using the Nernst equation. For example, reversal potential for potassium ions will be as follows:

$$E_{eq}, K^+ = \frac{RT}{zF} \ln \frac{[K^+]_o}{[K^+]_i};$$

where

- $E_{eq,}K^+$ is the equilibrium potential for potassium, measured in volts.
- R is the universal gas constant, equal to 8.314 joules·K^{-1}·mol^{-1}.
- T is the absolute temperature, measured in kelvins (= K = degrees Celsius + 273.15).
- z is the number of elementary charges of the ion in question involved in the reaction.
- F is the Faraday constant, equal to 96,485 coulombs·mol^{-1} or J·V^{-1}·mol^{-1}
- $[K^+]_o$ is the extracellular concentration of potassium, measured in mol·m^{-3} or mmol·l^{-1}
- $[K^+]_i$ is the intracellular concentration of potassium.

Apparently, even if two different ions have the same charge (ie. K^+ and Na^+), they can still have very different equilibrium potentials, provided their outside and/or inside concentrations differ. Take, for example, the equilibrium potentials of potassium and sodium in neurons. The potassium equilibrium potential *E*K is -84 mV with 5 mM potassium outside and 140 mM inside. The sodium equilibrium potential, on the other hand, E_{Na} is approximately +40 mV with approximately 12 mM sodium inside and 140 mM outside.

Resting potential and action potential are often referred as "potassium" and "sodium" potentials, respectively. This stems from the origin of the resting potential (proximity to the EK), and the origin (activation of sodium channels) and the peak amplitude of the action potential (proximity to the ENa).

Resting Membrane Potential

Relatively static membrane potential of quiescent cells is called resting membrane potential (or resting voltage), as opposed to the dynamic electrochemical phenomenona called action potential and graded membrane potential. Apart from the latter two, which occur in excitable cells (neurons, muscles, and some secretory cells in glands), membrane voltage in the non-excitable cells can also undergo changes in response to environmental or intracellular stimuli. For example, depolarization of the plasma membrane appears to be an important step in programmed cell death. In principle, there is no difference between resting membrane potential and dynamic voltage changes like action potential from biophysical point of view: all these phenomena are caused by specific changes in membrane permeabilities for potassium, sodium, calcium, and chloride, which in turn result from concerted changes in functional activity of various ion channels, ion pumps, exchangers, and transporters. Conventionally, resting membrane potential can be defined as a relatively stable, ground, value of transmembrane voltage in animal and plant cells.

Generation of resting membrane potential is explicitly explained by Goldman equation It is essentially the Nernst equation, in that it is based on the charges of the ions in question, as well as the difference between their inside and outside concentrations. However, it also takes into consideration the relative permeability of the plasma membrane to each ion in question.

$$E_m = \frac{RT}{F}\ln\left(\frac{P_K[K^+]_{out} + P_{Na}[Na^+]_{out} + P_{Cl}[Cl^-]_{in}}{P_K[K^+]_{in} + P_{Na}[Na^+]_{in} + P_{Cl}[Cl^-]_{out}}\right)$$

for the three monovalent ions most important to action potentials: potassium (K^+), sodium (Na^+), and chloride (Cl^-). Being an anion, the chloride terms are treated differently than the cation terms; the inside concentration is in the numerator, and the outside concentration is in the denominator, which is reversed from the cation terms. P_i stands for the permeability of the ion type i. If calcium ions are also considered, which are critically important for action potentials in muscles, the formula for the equilibrium potential becomes more complicated. The resting plasma membrane of the most animal cells is much more permeable to K^+, which results in the resting potential to be close to the potassium equilibrium potential.

The resting potential of a cell can be most thoroughly understood by thinking of it in terms of equilibrium potentials. In the example diagram here, the model cell was given only one permeant ion (potassium). In this case, the resting potential of this cell would be the same as the equilibrium potential for potassium.However, a real cell is more complicated, having permeabilities to many ions, each of which contributes to the resting potential. To understand better, consider a cell with only two permeant ions, potassium and sodium. Consider a case where these two ions have equal concentration gradients directed in opposite directions, and that the membrane permeabilities to both ions are equal. K^+ leaving the cell will tend to drag the membrane potential toward E_K. Na^+ entering the cell will tend to drag the membrane potential toward the reversal potential for sodium *E*Na. Since the permeabilities to both ions were set to be equal, the membrane potential will, at the end of the Na^+/K^+ tug-of-war, end up halfway between E_{Na} and E_K. As E_{Na} and E_K were equal but of opposite signs, halfway in between is zero, meaning that the membrane will rest at 0 mV.

Note that even though the membrane potential at 0 mV is stable, it is not an equilibrium condition because neither of the contributing ions are in equilibrium. Ions diffuse down their electrochemical gradients through ion channels, but the membrane potential is upheld by continual K^+ influx and Na^+ efflux via ion pumps. Such situation with similar permeabilities for counter-acting ions, like potassium and sodium in animal cells, can be extremely costly for the cell if these permeabilities are relatively large, as it takes a lot of ATP energy to pump the ions back. Because no real cell can afford such equal and large ionic permeabilities at rest, resting potential of animal cells is determined by predominant high permeability to potassium and adjusted to the required value by modulating sodium and chloride permeabilities and gradients.

A healthy animal cell Na^+ permeability is about 5% of the K permeability or even less, whereas the respective reversal potentials are +60 mV for sodium and -80 mV for potassium. Thus the membrane potential will not be right at E_K, but rather depolarized from E_K by an amount of approximately 5% of the 140 mV difference between E_K and E_{Na}. Thus, the cell's resting potential will be about -73 mV.

In a more formal notation, the membrane potential is the weighted average of each contributing ion's equilibrium potential (Goldman equation). The size of each weight is the relative permeability of each ion. In the normal case, where three ions contribute to the membrane potential:

$$E_m = \frac{PK^+}{P_{tot}} E_{K+} + \frac{PNa^+}{P_{tot}} E_{Na+} + \frac{PCl^-}{P_{tot}} ECl^-$$

where

- E_m is the membrane potential, measured in volts
- E_X is the equilibrium potential for ion X, also in volts
- P_X is the relative permeability of ion X in arbitrary units (e.g. siemens for electrical conductance)
- P_{tot} is the total permeability of all permeant ions, in this case $P_{tot} = PK^+ + PNa^+ + PCl^-$

It is important to understand that ionic and water permeability of a pure lipid bilayer is very small, and it is similarly negligible for ions of comparable size, such as Na^+ and

K^+. The cell membranes, however, contain a large number of ion channels, water channels (aquaporins), and various ionic pumps, exchangers, and transporters, which can selectively increase permeability of the membrane for different ions. The relatively high membrane permeability for potassium ions at resting potential results from inward-rectifier potassium ion channels which are open at negative voltages, and so called leak potassium conductances such as two-barrel open rectifier K^+ channel (ORK^+) which is locked in the open state irrespective of voltage. These potassium channels should not be confused with voltage-activated K^+ channels responsible for membrane repolarization during action potential.

Values of resting membrane potential in the most of the mature (differentiated) animal cells usually vary between E_K and around -40 mV. Resting voltage in the excitable cells capable of producing action potentials is usually balanced around -60 mV because more depolarized voltage would lead to spontaneous activation of voltage-activated sodium channels and generate action potential. Immature or not-differentiated cells demonstrate highly variable values of resting voltage usually significantly more positive than that in the differentiated cells In such cells, the resting potential value correlates well with the degree of differentiation: undifferentiated cells can demonstrate resting potential value as low as 0 mV.

Maintenance of resting potential can be very costly for a cell, especially when the cell function requires a rather depolarized value of membrane voltage. For example, resting potential in day light-adapted blowfly (*Calliphora vicina*) photoreceptors can be as high as -30 mV In insect photoreceptors depolarization is provided by light-activated TRP channels which cause fluctuations in membrane voltage in response to changing ambient light intensity. These changes in voltage then propagate as graded membrane responses to the synapses with a second-order neuron. At -30 mV, blowfly photoreceptor input resistance and membrane time constant can be as low as 10 MO and 1.5 ms, respectively, and the corner frequency of the voltage response power spectrum as high as 120 Hz. Such remarkably high corner frequency allows *Calliphora vicina* to produce the fastest functional responses ever recorded from an ocular photoreceptor This excellent visual ability, however, is very expensive metabolically, because such a low membrane resistance results from numerous open voltage-activated potassium and light-activated TRP channels, which, in turn, requires high level of Na^+/K^+-ATPase activity to maintain the proper ionic gradients. As a result, blowfly retina is one of the most, if not the most, energy demanding tissues in the fly both under dark- and light-adapted conditions. Maintenance of resting potential in such cells may cost more than 20% of overall cellular ATP.

On the other hand, high resting potential in the not-differentiated cells can be rather a great metabolic advantage, and not a burden for non-active cells such as stem cells. This apparent paradox is easily resolved by careful examination of the origin of that resting potential. Low-differentiated cells are characterized by extremely high input resistance which implies that leak and inward rectifier potassium channels, which are responsible for high potassium permeability at rest, as well as other leak conductances (cloride and sodium, for example), are not expressed at this stage of cell life. As an apparent result, potassium permeability becomes similar to that for sodium ions, which places resting potential in-between the reversal potentials for sodium and potassium as discussed above. And because all ionic permeabilities in such cells are virtually the basic ionic leaks of a lipid bilayer, very little metabolic cost may be associated with maintenance of resting potential in such cells.

Action Potential

Neurons communicate with other neurons, muscles, and organs via action potentials (APs), brief transient waveforms quickly "moving" along neuronal axons. The typical duration of an action potential registered with a pointed electrode is about 1 ms, which includes fast depolarization from the resting potential by means of opening of voltage-activated sodium channels, followed by slower repolarization of the membrane as a result of opening of voltage-activated potassium channels. After-hyperpolarization or "undershoot" is the final phase of an action potential which results from the activity of Na^+/K^+-ATPase (two K^+ ions in, three Na+ ions out per cycle of pumping results in the net one positive charge leaving the cell, i.e. one negative charge entering the cell), opening of calcium- and sodium-activated potassium channels, and deactivating delayed-rectifier potassium channels.

Action potential is initiated when membrane is depolarized above action potential activation threshold, which is approximately 20 mV above the resting potential level in neurons (-60 mV). In neurons *in vivo*, initial depolarization is caused by spatio-temporal summation of graded excitatory postsynaptic potentials (EPSPs), which is the "natural" mechanism of action potential initiation in neuronal networks. For example, it may require hundreds and thousands of EPSPs simultaneously or almost simultaneously converging on the neuron to evoke an action potential because a typical amplitude of an EPSP is 0.1 mV and the excitatory graded potentials are offset by their inhibitory counterparts, inhibitory postsynaptic potentials (IPSPs). Alternatively, action potentials can be initiated by external injection of a brief depolarizing current pulse *in vitro* and *in vivo*, during physiological experiments and in certain medical devices. Sodium and potassium channels are key components of AP generation and propagation. Voltage-activated sodium channels, which are predominantly closed at resting voltage levels, react to a depolarizing perturbation by further opening, first gradually and linearly, but then, beyond a certain threshold, in a robust avalanche-like manner. The principal mechanism of AP generation was discovered by Hodgkin and Huxley and discussed in detail elsewhere.

Inactivation of sodium channels is responsible for the so called "absolute refractory period" after action potential. During that period of an order of few milliseconds duration no consequtive AP can be evoked by no matter how large depolarization. During the *relative refractory period,* a sufficient number of sodium channels (but not all) have recovered that an action potential can be provoked, but only with a stimulus much stronger than usual. These refractory periods ensure that the action potential travels in only one direction along the axon

Action potentials usually originate at the axon hillock, where voltage-activated sodium channel density is the highest and their activation voltage threshold is the lowest, but they can be initiated in any part of neuron including dendrites and soma, if density of sodium channels allows it. Action potentials, originating from dendrites and soma have different shapes (broader in dendrites), and the critical amplitude of depolarizing perturbation (AP threshold level) changes as: dendrites > soma > axon hillock. APs usually propagate from axon hillock toward axonal synapses, but can also propagate back to soma and dendrites, although the biological significance and network calculation benefits of this phenomenon are not yet established.

Graded Membrane Potential

A graded membrane potential is a gradient of transmembrane potential difference along a length of cell membrane. Graded potentials are particularly important in neurons that lack action potentials, such as some types of retinal neurons. Graded potentials that depolarize the membrane, increasing the membrane potential above the resting potential are important as "triggering potentials" that can spread along the surface of neuronal cell bodies to axon initial segments and trigger action potentials. Graded potentials that hyperpolarize the membrane potential to values more negative than the resting potential can inhibit the generation of action potentials. Graded potentials can arise at either portions of cells that function as sensory receptors or at synapses that are activated by neurotransmitters. These two types of graded potentials are called receptor potentials or synaptic potentials. Graded potentials are distinct from action potentials in that graded potentials spread electric potential changes along cell membranes without activating the kind of constant magnitude propagating signal that is characteristic of the action potential. Graded potentials are highest at a source and decay with increasing distance from the source. Membrane potential is significantly important as far as normal body functions are to be maintained

From the viewoint of biophysics, there is nothing particularly special about the resting membrane potential. It is merely the membrane potential that results from the membrane permeabilities that predominate when the cell is resting. The above equation of weighted averages always applies, but the following approach may be easier to visualize. At any given moment, there are two factors for an ion that determine how much influence that ion will have over the membrane potential of a cell.

That ion's driving force and,

That ion's permeability.

Intuitively, this is easy to understand. If the driving force is high, then the ion is being "pushed" across the membrane hard (more correctly stated: it is diffusing in one direction faster than the other). If the permeability is high, it will be easier for the ion to diffuse across the membrane. But what are 'driving force' and 'permeability'?

- Driving force: the driving force is the net electrical force available to move that ion across the membrane. It is calculated as the difference between the voltage that the ion "wants" to be at (its equilibrium potential) and the actual membrane potential (E_m). So formally, the driving force for an ion = E_m - E_{ion}

- For example, at our earlier calculated resting potential of -73 mV, the driving force on potassium is 7 mV [(-73 mV) - (-80 mV) = 7 mV]. The driving force on sodium would be (-73 mV) - (60 mV) = -133 mV.
- Permeability: is simply a measure of how easily an ion can cross the membrane. It is normally measured as the (electrical) conductance and the unit, siemens, corresponds to 1 $C \cdot s^{-1} \cdot V^{-1}$, that is one charge per second per volt of potential.

So in a resting membrane, while the driving force for potassium is low, its permeability is very high. Sodium has a huge driving force, but almost no resting permeability. In this case, the math tells us that potassium carries about 20 times more current than sodium, and thus has 20 times more influence over E_m than does sodium.

However, consider another case—the peak of the action potential. Here permeability to Na is high and K permeability is relatively low. Thus the membrane moves to near E_{Na} and far from E_K.

The more ions are permeant, the more complicated it becomes to predict the membrane potential. However, this can be done using the Goldman-Hodgkin-Katz equation or the weighted means equation. By simply plugging in the concentration gradients and the permeabilities of the ions at any instant in time, one can determine the membrane potential at that moment. What the GHK equations says, basically, is that at any time, the value of the membrane potential will be a weighted average of the equilibrium potentials of all permeant ions. The "weighting" is the ions relative permeability across the membrane.

Effects and Implications

While cells expend energy to transport ions and establish a transmembrane potential, they use this potential in turn to transport other ions and metabolites such as sugar. The transmembrane potential of the mitochondria drives the production of ATP, which is the common currency of biological energy.

Cells may draw on the energy they store in the resting potential to drive action potentials or other forms of excitation. These changes in the membrane potential enable communication with other cells (as with action potentials) or initiate changes inside the cell, which happens in an egg when it is fertilized by a sperm.

In neuronal cells, an action potential begins with a rush of sodium ions into the cell through sodium channels, resulting in depolarization, while recovery involves an outward rush of potassium through potassium channels. Both these fluxes occur by passive diffusion.

7

Action Potential

In neurophysiology, the action potential is a self-regenerating wave of electrochemical activity that allows nerve cells to carry a signal over a distance. It is the primary electrical signal generated by nerve cells, and arises from changes in the permeability of the nerve cell's axonal membranes to specific ions. Action potentials (also known as nerve impulses or spikes) are pulse-like waves of voltage that travel along several types of cell membranes. The best-understood example of an action potential is generated on the membrane of the axon of a neuron, but also appears in other types of excitable cells, such as cardiac muscle cells, and even plant cells.

A typical action potential is initiated at the axon hillock when the membrane is depolarized sufficiently (i.e. when its voltage is increased sufficiently). As the membrane potential is increased, both the sodium and potassium ion channels begin to open. This increases both the inward sodium current and the balancing outward potassium current. For small voltage increases, the potassium current triumphs over the sodium current and the voltage returns to its normal resting value, typically -70 mV. However, if the voltage increases past a critical threshold, typically 15 mV higher than the resting value, the sodium current dominates. This results in a runaway condition whereby the positive feedback from the sodium current activates even more sodium channels. Thus, the cell "fires", producing an action potential.

Once initiated, the action potential travels through the axon. Since the axon is insulated, the action potential can travel through it without significant signal decay. Nevertheless, to ensure the signal does not fail, regularly spaced patches, called the nodes of Ranvier, help boost the signal. The process here resembles that at the axon hillock. The action potential depolarizes the membrane patch at the node of Ranvier, sparking another action potential. In effect, the action potential is created afresh at each node of Ranvier. The axon then branches along its length, and the action potentials travel down each branch. At this point, the axon sheds its insulation, and instead, the action potential is propagated by the voltage activated sodium channels. Here, the inward current may not quite suffice to trigger a new action potential in some of these branches. The action potential may thus fail Action potentials that do reach the ends of the axon generally cause the release of a neurotransmitter into the synaptic cleft. This may combine with other inputs to provoke a new action potential in the post-synaptic neuron or muscle cell.

The principal ions involved in an action potential are sodium and potassium cations; sodium ions enter the cell, and potassium ions leave, restoring equilibrium. Relatively few ions need to cross the membrane for the membrane voltage to change drastically. The ions exchanged during an action potential, therefore, make a negligible change in the interior and exterior ionic concentrations. The few ions that do cross are pumped out again by the continual action of the sodium–potassium pump, which, with other ion transporters, maintains the normal ratio of ion concentrations across the membrane. Calcium cations and chloride anions are involved in a few types of action potentials, such as the cardiac action potential and the action potential in the single-celled alga Acetabularia, respectively.

Electrical signals within biological organisms are generally driven by ions. The most important cations for the action potential are sodium (Na^+) and potassium. (K^+) Both of these are *monovalent* cations that carry a single positive charge. Action potentials can also involve calcium (Ca^{2+}) which is a *divalent* cation that carries a double positive charge. The chloride anion (Cl^-) plays a major role in the action potentials of some algae but plays a negligible role in the action potentials of most animals.

Ions cross the cell membrane under two influences: diffusion and electric fields. Let's start off with a simple example whereby two solutions are separated by a porous barrier. Let us further call these two solutions A and B. In this case, diffusion will ensure that they will eventually mix into equal solutions. This mixing occurs because of the difference in their concentrations. The region with high concentration will diffuse out towards the region with low concentration. To further the example, let solution A have 30 sodium ions and 30 chloride ions. Also, let solution B have only 20 sodium ions and 20 chloride ions. Assuming the barrier allows both types of ions to travel through it, then a steady state will be reached whereby both solutions have 25 sodium ions and 25 chloride ions. If, however, the porous barrier is selective to which ions are let through, then diffusion alone will not determine the resulting solution. Returning to the previous example, lets now construct a barrier that is only permeable to sodium ions. Since solution B has a lower concentration of both sodium and chloride, it will attract both ions from solution A. However, only sodium will travel through the barrier. This will result in an accumulation of sodium in solution B. Since sodium has a positive charge, this accumulation will make solution B more positive relative to solution A. Positive sodium ions will be less likely to travel to the now more positive B solution. This constitutes the second factor controlling ion flow, namely electric fields. The point at which this electric field completely counteracts the force due to diffusion is called the equilibrium potential. At this point, the net flow of this specific ion (in this case sodium) is zero.

Cell Membrane

Each neuron is encased in a cell membrane. This membrane is nearly impermeable to ions To transfer ions into, and out of the neuron, the membrane provides two structures. Ion pumps use the cell's energy to continuously move ions in and out. They create concentration differences (between the inside and outside of the neuron) by transporting ions against their concentration gradients (from regions of low concentration to regions of high concentration). The ion channels then use this concentration difference to transport ions down their concentration gradients (from regions of high concentration to regions of low concentration). However, unlike the continuous transport by the ion pumps, the transport by the ion channels is non continuous. They only open and close in response to signals from their environment. This transport of ions through the ion channels then changes the voltage of the cell membrane. These changes are what bring about an action potential. As an analogy, ion pumps play the role of the battery that allows a radio circuit (the ion channels) to transmit a signal (action potential).

Membrane Potential

The cell membrane acts as a barrier which prevents the inside solution (intracellular fluid) from mixing with the outside solution (extracellular fluid). These two solutions have different concentrations of their ions. Furthermore, this difference in concentrations leads to a difference in charge of the solutions. This creates a situation whereby one solution is more positive than the other. Therefore, positive ions will tend to gravitate towards the negative solution. Likewise, negative ions will tend to gravitate towards the positive solution. To quantify this property, one would like to somehow capture this relative positivity (or negativity). To do this, the outside solution is set as the zero voltage. Then the difference between the inside voltage and the zero voltage is determined. For example, if the outside voltage is 100 mV, and the inside voltage is 30

Ion channels can be classified by how they respond to their environment.For example, the ion channels involved in the action potential are *voltage-sensitive channels*; they open and close in response to the voltage across the membrane. *Ligand-gated channels* form another important class; these ion channels open and close in response to the binding of a ligand molecule, such as a neurotransmitter. Other ion channels open and close with mechanical forces. Still other ion channels—such as those of sensory neurons—open and close in response to other stimuli, such as light, temperature or pressure.

Ion Pumps

The ionic currents of the action potential flow in response to concentration differences of the ions across the cell membrane. These concentration differences are established by ion pumps, which are integral membrane proteins that carry out active transport, i.e., use cellular energy (ATP) to "pump" the ions against their concentration gradientSuch ion pumps take in ions from one side of the membrane (decreasing its concentration there) and release them on the other side (increasing its concentration there). The ion pump most relevant to the action potential is the sodium–potassium pump, which transports three sodium ions out of the cell and two potassium ions in Consequently, the concentration of potassium ions K^+ inside the neuron is roughly 20-fold larger than the outside concentration, whereas the sodium concentration outside is roughly ninefold larger than inside. Similarly, other ions have different concentrations inside and outside the neuron, such as calcium, chloride and magnesium.

Ion pumps influence the action potential only by establishing the relative ratio of intracellular and extracellular ion concentrations. The action potential mainly involves the opening and closing of ion channels, not ion pumps. If the ion pumps are turned off by removing their energy source, or by adding an inhibitor such as ouabain, the axon can still fire hundreds of thousands of action potentials before their amplitudes begin to decay significantly. In particular, ion pumps play no significant role in the repolarization of the membrane after an action potential.

Resting Potential

As described in the section Ions and the forces driving their motion, equilibrium or reversal potential of an ion is the value of transmembrane voltage at which the electric force generated by diffusional movement of the ion down its concentration gradient becomes equal to the molecular force of that diffusion. The equilibrium potential for any ion can be calculated using the nernst equation (*see Chapter 6*).

However, there is an equilibrium membrane potential E_m at which the *net* flow of all ions across the membrane is zero. This potential is calculated by the Goldman equation It is essentially the Nernst equation, in that it is based on the charges of the ions in question, as well as the difference between their inside and outside concentrations.

Generation of resting membrane potential is explicitly explained by Goldman equation. The resting plasma membrane of the most animal cells is much more permeable to K^+, which results in the resting potential V_{rest} to be close to the potassium equilibrium potentia.

It is important to realize, that ionic and water permeability of a pure lipid bilayer is very small, and it is similarly negligible for ions of comparable size, such as Na^+ and K^+. The cell membranes, however, contain a large number of ion channels, water channels (aquaporins), and various ionic pumps, exchangers, and transporters, which dramatically and selectively increase permeability of the membrane for different ions. The relatively high membrane permeability for potassium ions at resting potential results from Inward-rectifier potassium ion channels which are open at negative voltages, and so called leak potassium conductances such as open rectifier K^+ channel (ORK^+) which are locked in open state. These potassium channels should not be confused with voltage-activated K^+ channels responsible for membrane repolarization during action potential.

Action potentials arriving at the synapses of the upper right neuron stimulate currents in its dendrites; these currents depolarize the membrane at its axon hillock, provoking an action potential that propagates down the axon to its synaptic knobs, releasing neurotransmitter and stimulating the post-synaptic neuron.

Pacemaker Potentials

In the cases of neurotransmission and sensory neurons, action potentials result from an external stimulus. However, some excitable cells require no such stimulus to fire: they spontaneously depolarize their axon hillock and fire action potentials at a regular rate, like an internal clock. The voltage traces of such cells are known as pacemaker potentials The cardiac pacemaker cells of the sinoatrial node in the heart provide a good example Although such pacemaker potentials have a natural rhythm, it can be adjusted by external stimuli; for instance, heart rate can be altered by pharmaceuticals as well as signals from the sympathetic and parasympathetic nerves The external stimuli do not cause the cell's repetitive firing, but merely alter its timing. In some cases, the regulation of frequency can be more complex, leading to patterns of action potentials, such as bursting.

Phases

The course of the action potential can be divided into five parts: the rising phase, the peak phase, the falling phase, the undershoot phase, and finally the refractory period. During the rising phase the membrane potential depolarises (becomes more positive). The point at which depolarisation stops is called the peak phase. At this stage, the membrane potential reaches a maximum. Subsequent to this, there is a falling phase. During this stage the membrane potential hyperpolarises (becomes more negative). The undershoot phase is the point during which the membrane potential becomes temporarily more negatively charged than when at rest. Finally, the time during which a subsequent action potential is impossible or difficult to fire is called the refractory period, which may overlap with the other phases.

The course of the action potential is determined by two coupled effects. First, voltage-sensitive ion channels open and close in response to changes in the membrane voltage V_m. This changes the membrane's permeability to those ions Secondly, according to the Goldman equation, this change in permeability changes in the equilibrium potential E_m, and, thus, the membrane voltage V_m. Thus, the membrane potential affects the permeability, which then further affects the membrane potential. This sets up the possibility for positive feedback, which is a key part of the rising phase of the action potential. A complicating factor is that a single ion channel may have multiple internal "gates" that respond to changes in V_m in opposite ways, or at different rates For example, although raising V_m *opens* most gates in the voltage-sensitive sodium channel, it also *closes* the channel's "inactivation gate", albeit more slowly. Hence, when V_m is raised suddenly, the sodium channels open initially, but then close due to the slower inactivation.

The voltages and currents of the action potential in all of its phases were modeled accurately by Alan Lloyd Hodgkin and Andrew Huxley in 1952 for which they were awarded the Nobel Prize in Physiology or Medicine in 1963. However, their model considers only two types of voltage-sensitive ion channels, and makes several assumptions about them, e.g., that their internal gates open and close independently of one another. In reality, there are many types of ion channels and they do not always open and close independently.

Stimulation and Rising Phase

A typical action potential begins at the axon hillock with a sufficiently strong depolarization, e.g. a stimulus that increases V_m. This depolarization is often caused by the injection of extra sodium cations into the cell; these cations can come from a wide variety of sources, such as chemical synapses, sensory neurons or pacemaker potentials.

The initial membrane permeability to potassium is low, but much higher than that of other ions, making the resting potential close to E_K˜ -75 mV. The depolarization opens both the sodium and potassium channels in the membrane, allowing the ions to flow into and out of the axon, respectively. If the depolarization is small (say, increasing V_m from -70 mV to -60 mV), the outward potassium current overwhelms the inward sodium current and the membrane repolarizes back to its normal resting potential around -70 mV. However, if the depolarization is large enough, the inward sodium current increases more than the outward potassium current and a runaway condition (positive feedback) results: the more inward current there is, the more V_m increases, which in turn further increases the inward current A sufficiently strong depolarization (increase in V_m) causes the voltage-sensitive sodium channels to open; the increasing permeability to sodium drives V_m closer to the sodium equilibrium voltage E_{Na}˜ +55 mV. The increasing voltage in turn causes even more sodium channels to open, which pushes V_m still further towards E_{Na}. This positive feedback continues until the sodium channels are fully open and V_m is close to E_{Na} The sharp rise in V_m and sodium permeability correspond to the *rising phase* of the action potential.

The critical threshold voltage for this runaway condition is usually around -45 mV, but it depends on the recent activity of the axon. A membrane that has just fired an action potential cannot fire another one immediately, since the ion channels have not returned to their usual state. The period during which no new action potential can be fired is called the *absolute refractory period*. At longer times, after some but not all of the ion channels have recovered, the axon can be stimulated to produce another action potential, but only with a much stronger depolarization, e.g., -30 mV. The period during which action potentials are unusually difficult to provoke is called the *relative refractory period*.

Peak and Falling Phase

The positive feedback of the rising phase slows and comes to a halt as the sodium ion channels become maximally open. At the peak of the action potential, the sodium permeability is maximized and the membrane voltage V_m is nearly equal to the sodium equilibrium voltage E_{Na}. However, the same raised voltage that opened the sodium channels initially also slowly shuts them off, by closing their pores; the sodium channels become *inactivated* This lowers the membrane's permeability to sodium, driving the membrane voltage back down. At the same time, the raised voltage opens voltage-sensitive potassium channels; the increase in the membrane's potassium permeability drives V_m towards E_K Combined, these changes in sodium and potassium permeability cause V_m to drop quickly, repolarizing the membrane and producing the "falling phase" of the action potential.

Hyperpolarization ("undershoot")

The raised voltage opened many more potassium channels than usual, and these do not close right away when the membrane returns to its normal resting voltage. The potassium permeability of the membrane is transiently unusually high, driving the membrane voltage V_m even closer to the potassium equilibrium voltage E_K. Hence, there is an undershoot, a *hyperpolarization* in technical language, that persists until the membrane potassium permeability returns to its usual value.

Refractory Period

The opening and closing of the sodium and potassium channels during an action potential may leave some of them in a "refractory" state, in which they are unable to open again (inactivation) until the membrane potential returns to a sufficiently negative value for a long enough time. In the *absolute refractory period,* so many ion channels are refractory that no new action potential can be fired. Significant recovery (de-inactivation) requires that the membrane potential remain hyperpolarized for a certain length of time. In the *relative refractory period,* enough channels have recovered that an action potential can be provoked, but only with a stimulus much stronger than usual. These refractory periods ensure that the action potential travels in only one direction along the axon.

Propagation

The action potential generated at the axon hillock propagates as a wave along the axon The currents flowing inwards at a point on the axon during an action potential spread out along the axon, and depolarize the adjacent sections of its membrane. If sufficiently strong, this depolarization provokes a similar action potential at the neighboring membrane patches. This basic mechanism was demonstrated by Alan Lloyd Hodgkin in 1937. After crushing or cooling nerve segments and thus blocking the action potentials, he showed that an action potential arriving on one side of the block could provoke another action potential on the other, provided that the blocked segment was sufficiently short.

Once an action potential has occurred at a patch of membrane, the membrane patch needs time to recover before it can fire again. At the molecular level, this *absolute refractory period* corresponds to the time required for the voltage-activated sodium channels to recover from inactivation, i.e. to return to their closed state. There are many types of voltage-activated potassium channels in neurons, some of them inactivate fast (A-type currents) and some of them inactivate slowly or not inactivate at all; this variability guarantees that there will be always an available source of current for repolarization, even if some of the potassium channels are inactivated because of preceding depolarization. On the other hand, all neuronal voltage-activated sodium channels inactivate within several millisecond during strong depolarization, thus making following depolarization impossible until a substantial fraction of sodium channels is not returned to their closed state. Although it limits the frequency of firing, the absolute refractory period ensures that the action potential moves in only one direction along an axon. The currents flowing in due to an action potential spread out in both directions along the axon. However, only the unfired part of the axon can respond with an action potential; the part that has just fired is unresponsive until the action potential is safely out of range and cannot restimulate that part. In the usual orthodromic conduction, the action potential propagates from the axon hillock towards the synaptic knobs (the axonal termini); propagation in the opposite direction—known as antidromic conduction—is very rare. However, if a laboratory axon is stimulated in its middle, both halves of the axon are "fresh", i.e., unfired; then two action potentials will be generated, one traveling towards the axon hillock and the other traveling towards the synaptic knobs.

Myelin and Saltatory Conduction

The evolutionary need for the fast and efficient transduction of electrical signals in nervous system resulted in appearance of myelin sheaths around neuronal axons. Myelin is a multi-lamellar membrane which enwraps the axon in segments separated by intervals known as nodes of Ranvier, is produced by specialized cells, Schwann cells exclusively in the peripheral nervous system, and by oligodendrocytes exclusively in the central nervous system. Myelin sheath reduces membrane capacitance and increases membrane resistance in the inter-node intervals, thus allowing a fast, saltatory movement of action potentials from node to node Myelination is found mainly in vertebrates, but an analogous system has been discovered in a few invertebrates, such as some species of shrimp Not all neurons in vertebrates are myelinated; for example, axons of the neurons comprising autonomous (vegetative) nervous system are not myelinated in general.

Myelin prevents ions from entering or leaving the axon along myelinated segments. As a general rule, myelination increases the conduction velocity of action potentials and makes them more energy-efficient. Whether saltatory or not, the mean conduction velocity of an action potential ranges from 1 m/s to over 100 m/s, and generally increases with axonal diamete.

Action potentials cannot propagate through the membrane in myelinated segments of the axon. However, the current is carried by the cytoplasm, which is sufficient to depolarize the next 1 or 2 node of Ranvier. Instead, the ionic current from an action potential at one node of Ranvier provokes another action potential at the next node; this apparent "hopping" of the action potential from node to node is known as saltatory conduction. Although the mechanism of saltatory conduction was suggested in 1925 by Ralph Lillie, the first experimental evidence for saltatory conduction came from Ichiji Tasak and Taiji Takeuch and from Andrew Huxley and Robert Stämpfli By contrast, in unmyelinated axons, the action potential provokes another in the membrane immediately adjacent, and moves continuously down the axon like a wave.

Myelin has two important advantages: fast conduction speed and energy efficiency. For axons larger than a minimum diameter (roughly 1 micrometre), myelination increases the conduction velocity of an action potential, typically tenfold. Conversely, for a given conduction velocity, myelinated fibres are smaller than their unmyelinated counterparts. For example, action potentials move at roughly the same speed (25 m/s) in a myelinated frog axon and an unmyelinated squid giant axon, but the frog axon has a roughly 30-fold smaller diameter and 100-fold smaller cross-sectional area. Also, since the ionic currents are confined to the nodes of Ranvier, far fewer ions "leak" across the membrane, saving metabolic energy. This saving is a significant selective advantage, since the human nervous system uses approximately 20% of the body's metabolic energy.

The length of axons' myelinated segments is important to the success of saltatory conduction. They should be as long as possible to maximize the speed of conduction, but not so long that the arriving signal is too weak to provoke an action potential at the next node of Ranvier. In nature, myelinated segments are generally long enough for the passively propagated signal to travel for at least two nodes while retaining enough amplitude to fire an action potential at the second or third node. Thus, the safety factor of saltatory conduction is high, allowing transmission to bypass nodes in case of injury. However, action potentials may end prematurely in certain places where the safety factor is low, even in unmyelinated neurons; a common example is the branch point of an axon, where it divides into two axons.

Some diseases degrade myelin and impair saltatory conduction, reducing the conduction velocity of action potentials The most well-known of these is multiple sclerosis, in which the breakdown of myelin impairs coordinated movement.

Cable Theory

Cable theory's simplified view of a neuronal fiber. The connected RC circuits correspond to adjacent segments of a passive neurite. The extracellular resistances r_e (the counterparts of the intracellular resistances r_i) are not shown, since they are usually negligibly small; the extracellular medium may be assumed to have the same voltage everywhere.

The flow of currents within an axon can be described quantitatively by cable theory and its elaborations, such as the compartmental model. Cable theory was developed in

1855 by Lord Kelvin to model the transatlantic telegraph cable and was shown to be relevant to neurons by Hodgkin and Rushton in 1946. In simple cable theory, the neuron is treated as an electrically passive, perfectly cylindrical transmission cable, which can be described by a partial differential equation.

$$\tau \frac{\partial V}{\partial t} = \lambda^2 \frac{\partial^2 V}{\partial \chi^2} - V$$

where $V(x, t)$ is the voltage across the membrane at a time t and a position x along the length of the neuron, and where λ and t are the characteristic length and time scales on which those voltages decay in response to a stimulus. Referring to the circuit diagram above, these scales can be determined from the resistances and capacitances per unit length

$$t = r_m C_m$$

$$\lambda = \sqrt{\frac{r_m}{r_l}}$$

These time- and length-scales can be used to understand the dependence of the conduction velocity on the diameter of the neuron in unmyelinated fibres. For example, the time-scale t increases with both the membrane resistance r_m and capacitance c_m. As the capacitance increases, more charge must be transferred to produce a given transmembrane voltage (by the equation $Q=CV$); as the resistance increases, less charge is transferred per unit time, making the equilibration slower. Similarly, if the internal resistance per unit length r_i is lower in one axon than in another (e.g., because the radius of the former is larger), the spatial decay length λ becomes longer and the conduction velocity of an action potential should increase. If the transmembrane resistance r_m is increased, that lowers the average "leakage" current across the membrane, likewise causing λ to become longer, increasing the conduction velocity.

Termination

Chemical Synapses

Action potentials that reach the synaptic knobs generally cause a neurotransmitter to be released into the synaptic cleft. Neurotransmitters are small molecules that may open ion channels in the postsynaptic cell; most axons have the same neurotransmitter at all of their termini. The arrival of the action potential opens voltage-sensitive calcium channels in the presynaptic membrane; the influx of calcium causes vesicles filled with neurotransmitter to migrate to the cell's surface and release their contents into the synaptic cleft. This complex process is inhibited by the neurotoxins tetanospasmin and botulinum toxin, which are responsible for tetanus and botulism, respectively.

Electrical Synapses

A special case of a chemical synapse is the neuromuscular junction, in which the axon of a motor neuron terminates on a muscle fibre. In such cases, the released neurotransmitter is acetylcholine, which binds to the acetylcholine receptor, an integral membrane protein in the membrane (the *sarcolemma*) of the muscle fibre. However, the acetylcholine does not remain bound; rather, it dissociates and is hydrolyzed by the enzyme, acetylcholinesterase, located in the synapse. This enzyme quickly reduces the stimulus to the muscle, which allows the degree and timing of muscular contraction to be regulated delicately. Some poisons inactivate acetylcholinesterase to prevent this control, such as the nerve agents sarin and tabun, and the insecticides diazinon and malathion.

Cardiac Action Potentials

The cardiac action potential differs from the neuronal action potential by having an extended plateau, in which the membrane is held at a high voltage for a few hundred milliseconds prior to being repolarized by the potassium current as use. This plateau is due to the action of slower calcium channels opening and holding the membrane voltage near their equilibrium potential even after the sodium channels have inactivated.

The cardiac action potential plays an important role in coordinating the contraction of the heart. The cardiac cells of the sinoatrial node provide the pacemaker potential that synchronizes the heart. The action potentials of those cells propagate to and through the atrioventricular node (AV node), which is normally the only conduction pathway between the atria and the ventricles. Action potentials from the AV node travel through the bundle of His and thence to the Purkinje fibers Conversely, anomalies in the cardiac action potential—whether due to a congenital mutation or injury—can lead to human pathologies, especially arrhythmias. Several anti-arrhythmia drugs act on the cardiac action potential, such as quinidine, lidocaine, beta blockers, and verapamil.

Muscular Action Potentials

The action potential in a normal skeletal muscle cell is similar to the action potential in neurons. Action potentials result from the depolarization of the cell membrane (the sarcolemma), which opens voltage-sensitive sodium channels; these become inactivated and the membrane is repolarized through the outward current of potassium ions. The resting potential prior to the action potential is typically -90mV, somewhat more negative than typical neurons. The muscle action potential lasts roughly 2-4 ms, the absolute refractory period is roughly 1-3 ms, and the conduction velocity along the muscle is roughly 5 m/s. The action potential releases calcium ions that free up the tropomyosin and allow the muscle to contract. Muscle action potentials are provoked by the arrival of a pre-synaptic neuronal action potential at the neuromuscular junction, which is a common target for neurotoxins.

Plant Action Potentials

Plant and fungal cells are also electrically excitable. The fundamental difference to animal action potentials is, that the depolarization in plant cells is not accomplished by an uptake of positive sodium ions, but by release of negative *chloride* ions. Together with the following release of positive potassium ions, which is common to plant and animal action potentials, the action potential in plants infers, therefore, an osmotic loss of salt (KCl), whereas the animal action potential is osmotically neutral, when equal amounts of entering sodium and leaving potassium cancel each other osmotically. The interaction of electrical and osmotic relations in plant cells indicates an osmotic function of electrical excitability in the common, unicellular ancestors of plants and animals under changing salinity conditions, whereas the present function of rapid signal transmission is seen as a younger accomplishment of metazoan cells in a more stable osmotic environment . It must be assumed that the familiar signalling function of action potentials in some vascular plants (e.g. *Mimosa pudica*), arose independently from that in metazoan excitable cells.

TAXONOMIC DISTRIBUTION AND EVOLUTIONARY ADVANTAGES

Action potentials are found throughout multicellular organisms, including plants, invertebrates such as insects, and vertebrates such as reptiles and mammals. Sponges seem to be the main phylum of multicellular eukaryotes that does not transmit action potentials, although some studies have suggested that these organisms have a form of electrical signaling, too The resting potential, as well as the size and duration of the action potential, have not varied much with evolution, although the conduction velocity does vary dramatically with axonal diameter and myelination.

Experimental Methods

The study of action potentials has required the development of new experimental methods. The initial work, prior to 1955, focused on three goals: isolating signals from single neurons or axons, developing fast, sensitive electronics, and shrinking electrodes enough that the voltage inside a single cell could be recorded.

The first problem was solved by studying the giant axons found in the neurons of the squid genus Loligo. These axons are so large in diameter (roughly 1 mm, or 100-fold larger than a typical neuron) that they can be seen with the naked eye, making them easy to extract and manipulate However, the Loligo axons are not representative of all excitable cells, and numerous other systems with action potentials have been studied.

The second problem was addressed with the crucial development of the voltage clamp which permitted experimenters to study the ionic currents underlying an action potential in isolation, and eliminated a key source of electronic noise, the current IC associated with the capacitance C of the membrane. Since the current equals C times the rate of change of the transmembrane voltage Vm, the solution was to design a circuit that kept Vm fixed (zero rate of change) regardless of the currents flowing across the membrane. Thus, the current required to keep Vm at a fixed value is a direct reflection of the current flowing through the membrane. Other electronic advances included the use of Faraday cages and electronics with high input impedance, so that the measurement itself did not affect the voltage being measured.

The third problem, that of obtaining electrodes small enough to record voltages within a single axon without perturbing it, was solved in 1949 with the invention of the glass micropipette electrode, which was quickly adopted by other researchers Refinements of this method are able to produce electrode tips that are as fine as 100 Å (10 nm), which also confers high input impedance Action potentials may also be recorded with small metal electrodes placed just next to a neuron, with neurochips containing EOSFETs, or optically with dyes that are sensitive to Ca^{2+} or to voltage.

As revealed by a patch clamp electrode, an ion channel has two states: open (high conductance) and closed (low conductance).While glass micropipette electrodes measure the sum of the currents passing through many ion channels, studying the electrical properties of a single ion channel became possible in the 1970s with the development of the patch clamp by Erwin Neher and Bert Sakmann. For this they were awarded the Nobel Prize in Physiology or Medicine in 1991 Patch-clamping verified that ionic channels have discrete states of conductance, such as open, closed and inactivated.

Neurotoxins

Several neurotoxins, both natural and synthetic, are designed to block the action potential. Tetrodotoxin from the pufferfish and saxitoxin from the Gonyaulax (the dinoflagellate genus responsible for "red tides") block action potentials by inhibiting the voltage-sensitive sodium channel;similarly, dendrotoxin from the black mamba snake inhibits the voltage-sensitive potassium channel. Such inhibitors of ion channels serve an important research purpose, by allowing scientists to "turn off" specific channels at will, thus isolating the other channels' contributions; they can also be useful in purifying ion channels by affinity chromatography or in assaying their concentration. However, such inhibitors also make effective neurotoxins, and have been considered for use as chemical weapons. Neurotoxins aimed at the ion channels of insects have been effective insecticides; one example is the synthetic permethrin, which prolongs the activation of the sodium channels involved in action potentials. The ion channels of insects are sufficiently different from their human counterparts that there are few side effects in humans. Many other neurotoxins interfere with the transmission of the action potential's effects at the synapses, especially at the neuromuscular junction.

History

The role of electricity in the nervous systems of animals was first observed in dissected frogs by Luigi Galvani, who studied it from 1791 to 1797 Galvani's results stimulated Alessandro Volta to develop the Voltaic pile—the earliest known electric battery—with which he studied animal electricity (such as electric eels) and the physiological responses to applied direct-current voltages.

Scientists of the 19th century studied the propagation of electrical signals in whole nerves (i.e., bundles of neurons) and demonstrated that nervous tissue was made up of cells, instead of an interconnected network of tubes (a *reticulum*). Carlo Matteucci followed up Galvani's studies and demonstrated that cell membranes had a voltage across them and could produce direct current. Matteucci's work inspired the German physiologist, Emil du Bois-Reymond, who discovered the action potential in 1848. The conduction velocity of action potentials was first measured in 1850 by du Bois-Reymond's friend, Hermann von Helmholtz. To establish that nervous tissue was made up of discrete cells, the Spanish physician Santiago Ramón y Cajal and his students used a stain developed by Camillo Golgi to reveal the myriad shapes of neurons, which they rendered painstakingly. For their discoveries, Golgi and Ramón y Cajal were awarded the 1906 Nobel Prize in Physiology Their work resolved a long-standing controversy in the neuroanatomy of the 19th century; Golgi himself had argued for the network model of the nervous system.

The 20th century was a golden era for electrophysiology. In 1902 and again in 1912, Julius Bernstein advanced the hypothesis that the action potential resulted from a change in the permeability of the axonal membrane to ions Bernstein's hypothesis was confirmed by Ken Cole and Howard Curtis, who showed that membrane conductance increases during an action potential In 1907, Louis Lapique suggested that the action potential was generated as a threshold was crosse, what would be later shown as a product of the dynamical systems of ionic conductances. In 1949, Alan Hodgkin and Bernard Katz refined Bernstein's hypothesis by considering that the axonal membrane might have different permeabilities to different ions; in particular, they demonstrated the crucial role of the sodium permeability for the action potential This line of research culminated in the five 1952 papers of Hodgkin, Katz and Andrew Huxley, in which they applied the voltage clamp technique to determine the dependence of the axonal membrane's permeabilities to sodium and potassium ions on voltage and time, from which they were able to reconstruct the action potential quantitatively. Hodgkin and Huxley correlated the properties of their mathematical model with discrete ion channels that could exist in several different states, including "open", "closed", and "inactivated". Their hypotheses were confirmed in the mid-1970s and 1980s by Erwin Neher and Bert Sakmann, who developed the technique of patch clamping to examine the conductance states of individual ion channels. in the 21st century, researchers are beginning to understand the structural basis for these conductance states and for the selectivity of channels for their species of ion through the atomic-resolution crystal structures fluorescence distance measurements and cryo-electron microscopy studies.

Julius Bernstein was also the first to introduce the Nernst equation for resting potential across the membrane; this was generalized by David E. Goldman to the eponymous Goldman equation in 1943. The sodium–potassium pump was identified in 1957 and its properties gradually elucidated culminating in the determination of its atomic-resolution structure by X-ray crystallography. The crystal structures of related ionic pumps have also been solved, giving a broader view of how these molecular machines work.

Mathematical and computational models are essential for understanding the action potential, and offer predictions that may be tested against experimental data, providing a stringent test of a theory. The most important and accurate of these models is the Hodgkin-Huxley model, which describes the action potential by a coupled set of four ordinary differential equations (ODEs). Although the Hodgkin-Huxley model may be a simplification of a realistic nervous membrane, its complexity has inspired several even-more-simplified models such as the Morris-Lecar mode and the FitzHugh-Nagumo model both of which have only two coupled ODEs. The properties of the Hodgkin-Huxley and FitzHugh-Nagumo models and their relatives, such as the Bonhoeffer-van der Pol model have been well-studied within mathematics computation and electronics. More modern research has focused on larger and more integrated systems; by joining action-potential models with models of other parts of the nervous system (such as dendrites and synapses), researches can study neural computation and simple reflexes, such as escape reflexes and others controlled by central pattern generators.

8

Titration

Titration is a common laboratory method of quantitative chemical analysis that is used to determine the unknown concentration of a known reactant. Because volume measurements play a key role in titration, it is also known as volumetric analysis. A reagent, called the titrant of known concentration (a standard solution) and volume is used to react with a solution of the analyte or titrand whose concentration is not known. Using a calibrated burette to add the titrant, it is possible to determine the exact amount that has been consumed when the endpoint is reached. The endpoint is the point at which the titration is complete, as determined by an indicator This is ideally the same volume as the equivalence point - the volume of added titrant at which the number of moles of titrant is equal to the number of moles of analyte, or some multiple thereof (as in polyprotic acids). In the classic strong acid-strong base titration, the endpoint of a titration is the point at which the pH of the reactant is just about equal to 7, and often when the solution permanently changes color due to an indicator. There are however many different types of titrations.

Many methods can be used to indicate the endpoint of a reaction; titrations often use visual indicators (the reactant mixture changes colour). In simple acid-base titrations a pH indicator may be used, such as phenolphthalein, which becomes pink when a certain pH (about 8.2) is reached or exceeded. Another example is methyl orange, which is red in acids and yellow in alkali solutions.

Not every titration requires an indicator. In some cases, either the reactants or the products are strongly coloured and can serve as the "indicator". For example, an oxidation-reduction titration using potassium permanganate (pink/purple) as the titrant does not require an indicator. When the titrant is reduced, it turns colourless. After the equivalence point, there is excess titrant present. The equivalence point is identified from the first faint pink color that persists in the solution being titrated.

Due to the logarithmic nature of the pH curve, the transitions are, in general, extremely sharp; and, thus, a single drop of titrant just before the endpoint can change the pH significantly—leading to an immediate colour change in the indicator. There is a slight difference between the change in indicator colour and the actual equivalence point of the titration. This error is referred to as an indicator error, and it is indeterminate.

History and Etymology

The word "titration" comes from the Latin word *titalus*, meaning inscription or title. The French word *titre*, also from this origin, means rank. Titration, by definition, is the determination of rank or concentration of a solution with respect to water with a pH of 7 (which is the pH of pure H_2O under standard conditions).

The origins of volumetric analysis are in late-18th-century French chemistry. Francois Antoine Henri Descroizilles developed the first burette (which looked more like a graduated cylinder) in 1791. Joseph Louis Gay-Lussac developed an improved version of the burette that included a side arm, and coined the terms "pipette" and "burette" in an 1824 paper on the standardization of indigo solutions. A major breakthrough in the methodology and popularization of volumetric analysis was due to Karl Friedrich Mohr, who redesigned the burette by placing a clamp and a tip at the bottom, and wrote the first textbook on the topic, *Lehrbuch der chemisch-analytischen Titrirmethode* (*Textbook of analytical-chemical titration methods*), published in 1855.

Preparing a Sample for Titration

In a titration, both titrant and analyte are required to be in a liquid (solution) form. If the sample is not a liquid or solution, the samples must be dissolved. If the analyte is very concentrated in the sample, it might be useful to dilute the sample.

Although the vast majority of titrations are carried out in aqueous solution, other solvents such as glacial acetic acid or ethanol (in petrochemistry) are used for special purposes.

A measured amount of the sample can be given in the flask and then be dissolved or diluted. The mathematical result of the titration can be calculated directly with the measured amount. Sometimes the sample is dissolved or diluted beforehand, and a measured amount of the solution is used for titration. In this case the dissolving or diluting must be done accurately with a known coefficient because the mathematical result of the titration must be multiplied with this factor.

Many titrations require buffering to maintain a certain pH for the reaction. Therefore, buffer solutions are added to the reactant solution in the flask to maintain the pH of the solution.

Some titrations require "masking" of a certain ion. This can be necessary when two reactants in the sample would react with the titrant and only one of them must be analysed, or when the reaction would be disturbed or inhibited by this ion. In this case another solution is added to the sample, which "masks" the unwanted ion (for instance by a weak binding with it or even forming a solid insoluble substance with it).

Some redox reactions may require heating the solution with the sample and titration while the solution is still hot (to increase the reaction rate).

Procedure

A typical titration begins with a beaker or Erlenmeyer flask containing a precise volume of the reactant and a small amount of indicator, placed underneath a burette containing the reagent. By controlling the amount of reagent added to the reactant, it is possible to detect the point at which the indicator changes colour. As long as the indicator has been chosen correctly, this should also be the point where the reactant and reagent neutralize each other, and, by reading the scale on the burette, the volume of reagent can be measured.

As the concentration of the reagent is known, the number of moles of reagent can be calculated [(since *concentration = moles/volume*(*L*)]. Then, from the chemical equation involving the two substances, the number of moles present in the reactant can be found. Finally, by dividing the number of moles of reactant by its volume, the concentration is calculated.

Types of Titrations

Titrations can be classified by the type of reaction. Different types of titration reaction include:

- *Acid-base titrations* are based on the neutralization reaction between the analyte and an acidic or basic titrant. These most commonly use a pH indicator, a pH meter, or a conductance meter to determine the endpoint.

- *Redox titrations* are based on an oxidation-reduction reaction between the analyte and titrant. These most commonly use a potentiometer or a redox indicator to determine the endpoint. Frequently either the reactants or the titrant have a colour intense enough that an additional indicator is not needed.
- *Complexometric titrations* are based on the formation of a complex between the analyte and the titrant. The chelating agent EDTA is very commonly used to titrate metal ions in solution. These titrations generally require specialized indicators that form weaker complexes with the analyte. A common example is Eriochrome Black T for the titration of calcium and magnesium ions.
- *A form of titration* can also be used to determine the concentration of a virus or bacterium. The original sample is diluted (in some fixed ratio, such as 1:1, 1:2, 1:4, 1:8, etc.) until the last dilution does not give a positive test for the presence of the virus. This value, the titre, may be based on $TCID_{50}$, EID_{50}, ELD_{50}, LD_{50} or pfu. This procedure is more commonly known as an assay.
- *A zeta potential titration* characterizes heterogeneous systems, such as colloids. Zeta potential plays role of indicator. One of the purposes is determination of iso-electric point when surface charge becomes 0. This can be achieved by changing pH or adding surfactant. Another purpose is determination of the optimum dose of the chemical for flocculation or stabilization.

Measuring the Endpoint of a Titration

Different methods to determine the endpoint include:

- *pH indicator:* This is a substance that changes colour in response to a chemical change. An acid-base indicator (e.g., phenolphthalein) changes colour depending on the pH. Redox indicators are also frequently used. A drop of indicator solution is added to the titration at the start; when the colour changes the endpoint has been reached.

- *A potentiometer can also be used.* This is an instrument that measures the electrode potential of the solution. These are used for titrations based on a redox reaction; the potential of the working electrode will suddenly change as the endpoint is reached.
- *pH meter:* This is a potentiometer that uses an electrode whose potential depends on the amount of H+ ion present in the solution. (This is an example of an ion-selective electrode.) This allows the pH of the solution to be measured throughout the titration. At the endpoint, there will be a sudden change in the measured pH. It can be more accurate than the indicator method, and is very easily automated.
- *Conductance:* The conductivity of a solution depends on the ions that are present in it. During many titrations, the conductivity changes significantly. (For instance, during an acid-base titration, the H+ and OH- ions react to form neutral H_2O. This changes the conductivity of the solution.) The total conductance of the solution depends also on the other ions present in the solution (such as counter ions). Not all ions contribute equally to the conductivity; this also depends on the mobility of each ion and on the total concentration of ions (ionic strength). Thus, predicting the change in conductivity is harder than measuring it.
- *Colour change:* In some reactions, the solution changes colour without any added indicator. This is often seen in redox titrations, for instance, when the different oxidation states of the product and reactant produce different colours.
- *Precipitation:* If the reaction forms a solid, then a precipitate will form during the titration. A classic

example is the reaction between Ag+ and Cl- to form the very insoluble salt AgCl. This usually makes it difficult to determine the endpoint precisely. As a result, precipitation titrations often have to be done as "back" titrations.

- *An isothermal titration calorimeter* uses the heat produced or consumed by the reaction to determine the endpoint. This is important in biochemical titrations, such as the determination of how substrates bind to enzymes.
- *Thermometric titrimetry* is an extraordinarily versatile technique. This is differentiated from calorimetric titrimetry by the fact that the heat of the reaction (as indicated by temperature rise or fall) is not used to determine the amount of analyte in the sample solution. Instead, the endpoint is determined by *the rate of temperature change*.
- *Spectroscopy* can be used to measure the absorption of light by the solution during the titration, if the spectrum of the reactant, titrant or product is known. The relative amounts of the product and reactant can be used to determine the endpoint.
- *Amperometry* can be used as a detection technique (amperometric titration). The current due to the oxidation or reduction of either the reactants or products at a working electrode will depend on the concentration of that species in solution. The endpoint can then be detected as a change in the current. This method is most useful when the excess titrant can be reduced, as in the titration of halides with Ag^+. (This is handy also in that it ignores precipitates.)

Back Titration

The term back titration is used when a titration is done "backwards": instead of titrating the original analyte, one adds a known excess of a standard reagent to the solution, then titrates the excess. A back titration is useful if the endpoint of the reverse titration is easier to identify than the endpoint of the normal titration. They are also useful if the reaction between the analyte and the titrant is very slow.

Particular Uses

- As applied to biodiesel, titration is the act of determining the acidity of a sample of WVO by the dropwise addition of a known base to the sample while testing with pH paper for the desired pH=8.5 reading. By knowing how much base neutralizes an amount of WVO, we discern how much base to add to the entire batch.
- Titrations are a very common procedure held in *secondary education*, to assess a Chemistry Student's practical skills.
- Titrations in the *petrochemical or food industry* to define oils, fats or biodiesel and similar substances. An example procedure for all three can be found here.
- *Acid number:* an acid-base titration with colour indicator is used to determine the free fatty acid content. See also: pH of fatty acids.
- *Iodine number:* a redox titration with colour indication, which indicates the amount of unsaturated fatty acids.
- *Saponification value:* an acid-base back titration with colour indicator or potentiometric to get a hint about the average chain length of fatty acids in a fat.
- *Karl Fischer titration* a method to analyse trace amounts of water in a substance.

mV, then the difference is 70 mV. This difference is what is commonly referred to as the membrane potential.

Ion Channels

Ion channels are integral membrane proteins with a pore through which ions can travel between extracellular space and cell interior. Most channels are specific (selective) for one ion; for example, most potassium channels are characterized by 1000:1 selectivity ratio for potassium over sodium, though potassium and sodium ions have the same charge and differ only slightly in their radius. The channel pore is typically so small that ions must pass through it in the single-file order Channel pore can be either open or closed for ion passage, although a number of channels demonstrate various sub-conductance levels. When a channel is open, ions permeate through the channel pore down the transmembrane concentration gradient for that particular ion. Rate of ionic flow through the channel, i.e. single-channel current amplitude, is determined by the maximum channel conductance and electrochemical driving force for that ion, which is the difference between instantaneous value of the membrane potential and the value of the reversal potential.

The action potential is a manifestation of different ion channels opening and closing at different times.

All-atom figure of the open potassium channel, with the potassium ion shown in purple in the middle. When the channel is closed, the passage is blocked.

A channel may have several different states (corresponding to different conformations of the protein), but each such state is either open or closed. In general, closed states correspond either to a contraction of the pore—making it impassable to the ion—or to a separate part of the protein stoppering the pore. For example, the voltage-dependent sodium channel undergoes *inactivation*, in which a portion of the protein swings into the pore, sealing it. This inactivation shuts off the sodium current and plays a critical role in the action potential.

9

Voltammetry

Voltammetry is a category of electroanalytical methods used in analytical chemistry and various industrial processes. In voltammetry, information about an analyte is obtained by measuring the current as the potential is varied.

Three Electrode System

Voltammetry experiments investigate the half cell reactivity of an analyte. Most experiments control the potential (volts) of an electrode in contact with the analyte while measuring the resulting current (amperes).

To conduct such an experiment requires at least two electrodes. The working electrode, which makes contact with the analyte, must apply the desired potential in a controlled way and facilitate the transfer of electrons to and from the analyte. A second electrode acts as the other half of the cell. This second electrode must have a known potential with which to gauge the potential of the working electrode, furthermore it must balance the electrons added or removed by the working electrode. While this is a viable setup, it has a number of shortcomings. Most significantly, it is extremely difficult for an electrode to maintain a constant potential while passing current to counter redox events at the working electrode.

To solve this problem, the role of supplying electrons and referencing potential has been divided between two separate electrodes. The reference electrode is a half cell with a known reduction potential. Its only role is to act as reference in measuring and controlling the working electrodes potential and at no point does it pass any current. The auxiliary electrode passes all the current needed to balance the current observed at the working electrode. To achieve this current, the auxiliary will often swing to extreme potentials at the edges of the solvent window, where it oxidizes or reduces the solvent or supporting electrolyte. These electrodes, the working, reference, and auxiliary make up the modern three electrode system.

There are many systems which have more electrodes, but their design principles are generally the same as the three electrode system. For example, the rotating ring-disk electrode has two distinct and separate working electrodes, a disk and a ring, which can be used to scan or hold potentials independently of each other. Both of these electrodes are balanced by a single reference and auxiliary combination for an over all four electrode design. More complicated experiments may add working electrodes as required and at times reference or auxiliary electrodes.

In practice it can be very important to have a working electrode with known dimensions and surface characteristics. As a result, it is common to clean and polish working electrodes regularly. The auxiliary electrode can be almost anything as long as it doesn't react with the bulk of the anaylte solution and conducts well. The reference is the most complex of the three electrodes, there are a variety of standards used and its worth investigating elsewhere. For non-aqueous work, IUPAC recommends the use of the ferrocene/ferrocenium couple as an internal standard. In most voltammetry experiments a bulk electrolyte (also known as supporting electrolyte) is used to minimize solution resistance. It can be possible to run an experiment without an bulk electrolyte but the added resistance greatly reduces accuracy of the results. In the case of room temperature ionic liquids the solvent can act as the electrolyte.

Theory

The Nernst equation is fundamental to voltammetry and can be used for a reversible reaction. In this equation the R represents the reduced species and O the oxidized.

$$E = E^0 - \frac{RT}{nF} \ln \frac{c_R^0}{c_O^0}$$

R = molar gas constant

T = absolute temperature

n = number of electrons transferred (as determined by the stoichiometry of the cell reaction)

F = Faraday constant

E = applied potential

E^0 = standard reduction potential

Another useful equation in voltammetry is the Butler-Volmer equation. This equation represents the relationship between concentration, current, and potential.

$$\frac{i}{nFA} = k^0 \left\{ c_o^0 \exp[-\alpha\theta] - c_R^0 \exp[(1-\alpha)\theta] \right\}$$

$\theta = nF(E - E0) / RT$

k^0 = heterogeneous rate constant

α = transfer coefficient

A = area of the electrode

i = current

n = number of electrons transferred

Types of Voltammetry

- Linear sweep voltammetry
- Staircase voltammetry
- Squarewave voltammetry
- *Cyclic voltammetry* - A voltammetric method that can be used to determine diffusion coefficients and half cell reduction potentials.
- *Anodic stripping voltammetry* - A quantitative, analytical method for trace analysis of metal cations. The analyte is deposited (electroplated) onto the working electrode during a deposition step, and then oxidized during the stripping step. The current is measured during the stripping step.
- *Cathodic stripping voltammetry* - A quantitative, analytical method for trace analysis of anions. A positive potential is applied, oxidizing the mercury electrode and forming insoluble precipitates of the anions. A negative potential then reduces (strips) the deposited film into solution.
- *Adsorptive stripping voltammetry* - A quantitative, analytical method for trace analysis. The analyte is deposited simply by adsorption on the electrode surface (i.e., no electrolysis), then electrolyzed to give the analytical signal. Chemically modified electrodes are often used.
- Alternating Current Voltammetry
- *Polarography* - a subclass of voltammetry where the working electrode is a dropping mercury electrode (DME), useful for its wide cathodic range and renewable surface.
- *Rotated electrode voltammetry* - A hydrodynamic technique in which the working electrode, usually a rotating disk electrode (RDE) or rotating ring-disk electrode (RRDE),

is rotated at a very high rate. This technique is useful for studying the kinetics and electrochemical reaction mechanism for a half reaction.

- Normal Pulse Voltammetry
- Differential pulse voltammetry
- Chronoamperometry

History

The beginning of voltammetry was facilitated by the discovery of polarography in 1922 by the Nobel Prize winning chemist Jaroslav Heyrovský. Early voltammetric techniques had many problems, limiting their viability for everyday use in analytical chemistry. The 1960s and 1970s saw many advances in the theory and instrumentation of all voltammetric methods. These advancements improved sensitivity and created new analytical methods. Industry responded with the production of cheaper instruments that could be effectively used in routine analytical work.

Applications

Voltametric sensors: A number of voltammetric systems are produced commercially for the determination of specific species that are of interest in industry and research. These devices are sometimes called electrodes but are, in fact, complete voltammetric cells and are better referred to as sensors.

The oxygen electrode: The determination of dissolved oxygen in a variety of aqueous environments, such as sea water, blood, sewage, effluents from chemical plants, and soils is of tremendous importance to industry, biomedical and environmental research, and clinical medicine. One of the most common and convenient methods for making such measurements is with the Clark oxygen sensor, which was patented by L.C. Clark, Jr. in 1956.

Cyclic Voltammetry

Cyclic voltammetry or CV is a type of potentiodynamic electrochemical measurement. In a cyclic voltammetry experiment the working electrode potential is ramped linearly versus time like linear sweep voltammetry. Cyclic voltammetry takes the experiment a step farther than linear sweep voltammetry which ends when it reaches a set potential. When cyclic voltammetry reaches a set potential, the working electrode's potential ramp is inverted. This inversion can happen multiple times during a single experiment. The current at the working electrode is plotted versus the applied voltage to give the cyclic voltammogram trace. Cyclic voltammetry is generally used to study the electrochemical properties of an analyte in solution

Experimental Method

In cyclic voltammetry, the electrode potential ramps linearly versus time as shown. This ramping is known as the experiment's scan rate (V/s). The potential is measured between the reference electrode and the working electrode and the current is measured between the working electrode and the counter electrode. This data is then plotted as current (*i*) vs. potential (*E*). As the waveform shows, the forward scan produces a current peak for any analytes that can be reduced (or oxidized depending on the initial scan direction) through the range of the potential scanned. The current will increase as the potential reaches the reduction potential of the analyte, but then falls off as the concentration of the analyte is depleted close to the electrode surface. If the redox couple is reversible then when the applied potential is reversed, it will reach the potential that will reoxidize the product formed in the first reduction reaction, and produce a current of reverse polarity from the forward scan. This oxidation peak will usually have a similar shape to the reduction peak. As a result, information about the redox potential and electrochemical reaction rates of the compounds are obtained.

For instance if the electronic transfer at the surface is fast and the current is limited by the diffusion of species to the electrode surface, then the current peak will be proportional to the square root of the scan rate. This relationship is described by the Cottrell equation.

Characterization

The utility of cyclic voltammetry is highly dependent on the analyte being studied. The analyte has to be redox active within the experimental potential window. It is also highly desirable for the analyte to display a reversible wave. A reversible wave is when an analyte is reduced or oxidized on a forward scan and is then reoxidized or rereduced in a predictable way on the return scan as shown in the first figure.

Reversible peaks have a distinct absolute potential difference between the reduction (E_{pc}) and oxidation peak (E_{pa}). In an ideal system $|E_{pc}-E_{pa}|$ would be 59 mV for a 1 electron process and 30 mV for a 2 electron process. In addition the ratio of the currents passed at reduction (i_{pc}) and end oxidation (i_{pa}) is near unity ($1 = i_{pa}/i_{pc}$) for a reversible peaks.

When such reversible peaks are observed thermodynamic information in the form of half cell potential $E^0_{½}$ can be determined. When waves are semi-reversible such as when i_{pa}/i_{pc} is less than or greater than 1, it can be possible to determine even more information especially kinetic processes like following chemical reaction.

When waves are non-reversible it is impossible to determine what their thermodynamic $E^0_{½}$ is with cyclic voltammetry. This $E^0_{½}$ can be determined however it often requires equal quantities of the analyte in both oxidation states. When a wave is non-reversible cyclic voltammetry can not determine if the wave is at its thermodynamic potential or shift to a more extreme potential by some form of overpotential. The couple could be irreversible because of a following chemical process, a common example for transition metals is a shift in the geometry of the coordination sphere. If this is the case, then higher scan rates may show a reversible wave. It is also possible that the wave is irreversible due to a physical process most commonly some form of precipitation as discussed below. Some speculation can be made in regards to irreversible waves however they are generally outside the scope of cyclic voltammetry.

Experimental Setup

The method uses a reference electrode, working electrode, and counter electrode which in combination are sometimes referred to as a three-electrode setup. Electrolyte is usually added to the test solution to ensure sufficient conductivity. The combination of the solvent, electrolyte and specific working electrode material determines the range of the potential.

Electrodes are static and sit in unstirred solutions during cyclic voltammetry. This "still" solution method results in cyclic voltammetry's characteristic diffusion controlled peaks. This method also allows a portion of the analyte to remain after reduction or oxidation where it may display further redox activity. Stirring the solution between cyclic voltammetry traces is important as to supply the electrode surface with fresh analyte for each new experiment. The solubility of an analyte can change drastically with its over all charge. Since cyclic voltammetry usually alters the charge of the analyte it is common for reduced or oxidized analyte to precipitate out onto the electrode. This layering of analyte can insulate the electrode surface, display its own redox activity in subsequent scans, or at the very least alter the electrode surface. For this and other reasons it is often necessary to clean electrodes between scans.

Common materials for working electrodes include glassy carbon, platinum, and gold. These electrodes are generally encased in a rod of inert insulator with a disk exposed at one end. A regular working electrode has a radius within an order of magnitude of 1 mm. Having a controlled surface area with a defined shape is important for interpreting cyclic voltammetry results.

To run cyclic voltammetry experiments at high scan rates a regular working electrode is insufficient. High scan rates create peaks with large currents and increased resistances which result in distortions. Ultra-micro-electrodes can be used to minimize the current and resistance.

The counter electrode, also known as the auxiliary or second electrode, can be any material which conducts easily and won't react with the bulk solution. Reactions occurring at the counter electrode surface are unimportant as long as it continues to conduct current well. To maintain the observed current the counter electrode will often oxidize or reduce the solvent or bulk electrolyte.

Reference electrodes are a complex subject and worth investigating elsewhere.

Variations

In some experiments an electroactive species is fixed to the surface of the electrode, for instance in microparticle voltammetry. Potentiodynamic techniques also exist that add low-amplitude ac perturbation to a potential ramp and measure variable response in a single frequency (ac voltammetry) or in many frequencies simultaneously (potentiodynamic electrochemical impedance spectroscopy). The response in alternating current is two-dimensional – it is characterised by amplitude and phase. The amplitude and phase depend differently on frequency for constituents of ac response attributed to different processes (charge transfer, diffusion, double layer charging, etc.). Frequency response analysis enables simultaneous monitoring of the various processes that contribute to the potentiodynamic ac response of electrochemical system.

Distinctions

Cyclic voltammetry is not a hydrodynamic technique. In a hydrodynamic technique flow is achieved at the electrode surface by stirring the solution, pumping the solution, or rotating the electrode as is the case with rotating disk electrodes and rotating ring-disk electrodes. These techniques target steady state conditions which appear the same scanned from the positive or the negative, thus limiting them to linear sweep voltammetry.

10

Electrolysis

In chemistry and manufacturing, electrolysis is a method of separating chemically bonded compounds by passing an electric current through them. Electrolysis is commercially highly important as a stage in the separation of elements from naturally-occurring sources such as ores using an electrolytic cell.

History

- 1800 - William Nicholson and Johann Ritter decomposed water into hydrogen and oxygen.
- 1807 - Potassium, Sodium, Barium and Magnesium were discovered by Sir Humphry Davy using electrolysis.
- 1886 - Fluorine was discovered by Henri Moissan using electrolysis.
- 1886 - Hall-Héroult process developed for making aluminium.
- 1890 - Castner-Kellner process developed for making sodium hydroxide.

Overview

Electrolysis is the passage of an electric current through an ionic substance that is either molten or dissolved in a suitable solvent, resulting in chemical reactions at the electrodes and separation of materials.

The main components required to achieve electrolysis are:

- A liquid containing mobile ions - an electrolyte.
- An external source of direct electric current.
- Two solid rods or plates known as electrodes.

The components perform the following roles in the electrolysis process:

- The mobile ions are the carriers of electrical current in the liquid (electrolyte). If the ions are not mobile, as in a solid salt then electrolysis cannot occur.
- The externally supplied direct electric current supplies the energy necessary to create or discharge the ions in the liquid or solution. Electric current is carried by electrons in the external circuit.
- The electrodes provide the physical interface between the electrical circuit providing the energy to achieve the electrolysis.
- The electrolyte containing the ionic materials that are to be separated.
- The electrodes must be able to conduct electricity. Electrodes of metal, graphite and semiconductor material are widely used. Choice of suitable electrode depends on:
- Chemical reactivity between the electrode and electrolyte.
- Cost of manufacture of the electrode.

Ancillary practical components to achieve electrolysis include:

- Vessels to supply, contain and remove the reactants and products.
- Electrical Circuitry

Process of Electrolysis

The key process of electrolysis is the interchange of atoms and ions by the removal or addition of electrons from the external circuit. The required products of electrolysis are in some different physical state from the electrolyte and can be removed by some physical process. For example, in the electrolysis of brine to produce hydrogen and chlorine, the products are gaseous. These gaseous products bubble from the electrolyte and are collected.

A liquid containing mobile ions (electrolyte) is produced by:

- Solvation or reaction of an ionic compound with a solvent (such as an acid) to produce mobile ions
- An ionic compound is melted (fused) by heating.

An electrical potential is applied across a pair of electrodes immersed in the electrolyte.

Each electrode attracts ions that are of the opposite charge. Positively-charged ions (cations) move towards the electron-providing (negative) cathode, whereas negatively-charged ions (anions) move towards the positive anode.

At the electrodes, electrons are absorbed or released by the atoms and ions. Those atoms that gain or lose electrons to become charged ions pass into the electrolyte. Those ions that gain or lose electrons to become uncharged atoms separate from the electrolyte. The formation of uncharged atoms from ions is called discharging.

The energy required to cause the ions to migrate to the electrodes, and the energy to cause the change in ionic state, is provided by the external source of electrical potential.

Oxidation and Reduction at the Electrodes

Oxidation of ions or neutral molecules occurs at the anode, and the reduction of ions or neutral molecules occurs at the cathode. For example, it is possible to oxidize ferrous ions to ferric ions at the anode:

$$Fe_{aq}^{2+} \rightarrow \mathrm{Fe}_{aq}^{3+} + e^{-}$$

It is also possible to reduce ferricyanide ions to ferrocyanide ions at the cathode

$$\mathrm{Fe(CN)}_6^{3-} + e^{-} \rightarrow \mathrm{Fe(CN)}_6^{4-}$$

Neutral molecules can also react at either electrode. For example: p-Benzoquinone can be reduced to hydroquinone at the cathode.

In the last example, H^+ ions (hydrogen ions) also take part in the reaction, and are provided by an acid in the solution, or the solvent itself (water, methanol etc). Electrolysis reactions involving H^+ ions are fairly common in acidic solutions. In alkaline solutions, reactions involving OH^- (hydroxide ions) are common.

The substances oxidised or reduced can also be the solvent (usually water) or the electrodes. It is possible to have electrolysis involving gases.

Energy Changes during Electrolysis

The amount of electrical energy that must be added equals the change in Gibbs free energy of the reaction plus the losses in the system. The losses can (in theory) be arbitrarily close to zero, so the maximum thermodynamic efficiency equals the enthalpy change divided by the free energy change of the reaction. In most cases, the electric input is larger than the enthalpy change of the reaction, so some energy is released in the form of heat. In some cases, for instance, in the electrolysis of steam into hydrogen and oxygen at high temperature, the opposite is true. Heat is absorbed from the surroundings, and the heating value of the produced hydrogen is higher than the electric input.

Related Techniques

The following techniques are related to electrolysis:

- Gel electrophoresis is an electrolysis using a gel solvent. It is used to separate substances, such as DNA strands, based on their electrical charge.
- Electrochemical cells, including the hydrogen fuel cell, utilise differences in Standard electrode potential in order to generate an electrical potential from which useful power can be extracted. Although related via the interaction of ions and electrodes, electrolysis and the operation of electrochemical cells are quite distinct. A chemical cell should not be thought of as performing "electrolysis in reverse".

Faraday's Laws of Electrolysis

First Law of Electrolysis

In 1832, Michael Faraday reported that the quantity of elements separated by passing an electrical current through a molten or dissolved salt is proportional to the quantity of electric charge passed through the circuit. This became the basis of the first law of electrolysis:

$$m = kog$$

Second Law of Electrolysis

Faraday also discovered that the mass of the resulting separated elements is directly proportional to the atomic masses of the elements when an appropriate integral divisor is applied. This provided strong evidence that discrete particles of matter exist as parts of the atoms of elements.

Industrial Uses

- Production of aluminium, lithium, sodium, potassium, magnesium
- Coulometric techniques can be used to determine the amount of matter transformed during electrolysis by measuring the amount of electricity required to perform the electrolysis.
- Production of chlorine and sodium hydroxide.
- Production of sodium chlorate and potassium chlorate.
- Production of perfluorinated organic compounds such as trifluoroacetic acid.
- Production of electrolytic copper as a cathode, from refined copper of lower purity as an anode.

Electrolysis has many other uses:

- Electrometallurgy is the process of reduction of metals from metallic compounds to obtain the pure form of metal using electrolysis. For example, sodium hydroxide in its molten form is separated by electrolysis into sodium and oxygen, both of which have important chemical uses. (Water is produced at the same time.)
- Anodization is an electrolytic process that makes the surface of metals resistant to corrosion. For example, ships are saved from being corroded by oxygen in the water by this process. The process is also used to decorate surfaces.
- A battery works by the reverse process to electrolysis. Humphry Davy found that lithium acts as an electrolyte and provides electrical energy.
- Production of oxygen for spacecraft and nuclear submarines.
- Electroplating is used in layering metals to fortify them. Electroplating is used in many industries for functional or decorative purposes, as in vehicle bodies and nickel coins.

- Production of hydrogen for fuel, using a cheap source of electrical energy. Electrolytic Etching of metal surfaces like tools or knives with a permanent mark or logo.

Electrolysis is also used in the cleaning and preservation of old artifacts. Because the process separates the non-metallic particles from the metallic ones, it is very useful for cleaning old coins and even larger objects.

Competing Half-reactions in Solution Electrolysis

Using a cell containing inert platinum electrodes, electrolysis of aqueous solutions of some salts leads to reduction of the cations (e.g. metal deposition with e.g. zinc salts) and oxidation of the anions (e.g. evolution of bromine with bromides). However with salts of some metals [e.g. sodium) hydrogen is evolved at the cathode and for salts containing some anions (e.g. sulfate (SO_4^{2-})] oxygen is evolved at the anode, and in both cases this is due to water being reduced to form hydrogen or oxidised to form oxygen. In principle the voltage required to electrolyse a salt solution can be derived from the standard electrode potential for the reactions at the anode and cathode. The standard electrode potential is directly related to the Gibb's free energy, ΔG, for the reactions at each electrode and refers to an electrode with no current flowing.

Using the Nernst equation the electrode potential can be calculated for a specific concentration of ions, temperature and the number of electrons involved. For pure water (pH 7):

- the electrode potential for the reduction producing hydrogen is -0.41 V.
- the electrode potential for the oxidation producing oxygen is +0.82 V.

Comparable figures calculated in a similar way, for 1M zinc bromide, $ZnBr_2$, are -0.76 V for the reduction to Zn metal and +1.07 V for the oxidation producing bromine. The conclusion from these figures is that hydrogen should be produced at the cathode and oxygen at the anode from the electrolysis of water which is at variance with the experimental observation that zinc metal is deposited and bromine is produced. The explanation is that these calculated potentials only indicate the thermodynamically preferred reaction. In practice many other factors have to be taken into account such as the kinetics of some of the reaction steps involved. These factors together mean that a higher potential is required for the reduction and oxidation of water than predicted, and these are termed overpotentials. Experimentally it is known that overpotentials depend on the design of the cell and the nature of the the electrodes.

For the electrolysis of neutral (pH 7) sodium chloride, the reduction of sodium ion is thermodynamically very difficult and water is reduced evolving hydrogen leaving hydroxide ions in solution. At the anode the oxidation of chlorine is observed rather than the oxidation of water since the overpotential for the oxidation of chloride to chlorine is lower than the overpotential for the oxidation of water to oxygen. The hydroxide ions and dissolved chlorine gas react further to form hypochlorous acid. The aqueous solutions resulting from this process is called electrolyzed water and is used as a disinfectant and cleaning agent.

ELECTROLYSIS OF WATER

Electrolysis of water is the decomposition of water (H_2O) into oxygen (O_2) and hydrogen gas (H_2) due to an electric current being passed through the water. This electrolytic process is used in some industrial applications when hydrogen is needed.

Principle

An electrical power source is connected to two electrodes, or two plates, (typically made from some inert metal such as platinum or stainless steel) which are placed in the water. Hydrogen will appear at the cathode (the negatively charged electrode, where electrons are pumped into the water), and oxygen will appear at the anode (the positively charged electrode). The generated amount of hydrogen is twice the amount of oxygen, and both are proportional to the total electrical charge that was sent through the water.

Electrolysis of pure water is very slow, and can only occur due to the self-ionization of water. Pure water has an electrical conductivity about one millionth that of seawater. It is sped up dramatically by adding an electrolyte (such as a salt, an acid or a base).

Historically, the first known electrolysis of water was done by William Nicholson and Anthony Carlisle in about 1800.

Equations

In the water at the negatively charged cathode, a reduction reaction takes place, with electrons (e-) from the cathode being given to hydrogen cations to form hydrogen gas (the half reaction balanced with acid):

Cathode (reduction): $2H^+(aq) + 2e^- = H_2(g)$

At the positively charged anode, an oxidation reaction occurs, generating oxygen gas and giving electrons to the cathode to complete the circuit:

Anode (oxidation): $2H_2O(l) = O_2(g) + 4H^+(\mathrm{aq}) + 4e^-$

The same half reactions can also be balanced with base as listed below. Not all half reactions must be balanced with acid or base. Many do like the oxidation or reduction of water listed here. To add half reactions they must both be balanced with either acid or base.

Cathode (reduction): $2H_2O(l) + 2e^- = H_2(g) + 2OH^-(aq)$

Anode (oxidation): $4OH^-(aq) = O_2(g) + 2H_2O(l) + 4e^-$

Combining either half reaction pair yields the same overall decomposition of water into oxygen and hydrogen:

Overall reaction: $2H_2O(l) = 2H_2(g) + O_2(g)$

The number of hydrogen molecules produced is thus twice the number of oxygen molecules. Assuming equal temperature and pressure for both gases, the produced hydrogen gas has therefore twice the volume of the produced oxygen gas. The number of electrons pushed through the water is twice the number of generated hydrogen molecules and four times the number of generated oxygen molecules.

Thermodynamics of the Process

Decomposition of pure water into hydrogen and oxygen at standard temperature and pressure is not favorable in thermodynamical terms. This is because, E(cell) = E(Oxidation) + E(Reduction). If E(cell) < 0, reaction is not favourable.

Anode (oxidation):

$$2H_2O(l) \rightarrow O_2(g) + 4H^+(aq) + 4e^- E_{oX} = -1.23V$$

Cathode (reduction):

$$2H^+(aq) + 4e^- \rightarrow H_2(g) E_{red} = 0.00V$$

Thus, the standard potential of the water electrolysis cell is -1.23 V at 25 °C from the Nernst Equation.

The negative voltage indicates the Gibbs free energy for electrolysis of water is greater than zero for these reactions. This can be found using the G=-nFE equation from chemical kinetics, where n is the moles of electrons and F is the Faraday constant. The reaction cannot occur without adding necessary energy, usually supplied by an external electrical power source.

Electrolyte Selection

If the above described processes occur in pure water, H^+ cations will accumulate at the anode and OH^- anions will accumulate at the cathode. This can be verified by adding a pH indicator to the water: the water near the anode is acidic while the water near the cathode is basic. These charged ions will repel the further flow of electricity until they have diffused away, a slow process. This is why pure water conducts electricity poorly and why electrolysis of pure water proceeds slowly.

If a water-soluble electrolyte is added, the conductivity of the water rises considerably. The electrolyte disassociates into cations and anions; the anions rush towards the anode and neutralize the buildup of positively charged H+ there; similarly, the cations rush towards the cathode and neutralize the buildup of negatively charged OH- there. This allows the continued flow of electricity.

Care must be taken in choosing an electrolyte, since an anion from the electrolyte is in competition with the hydroxide ions to give up an electron. An electrolyte anion with less standard electrode potential than hydroxide will be oxidized instead of the hydroxide, and no oxygen gas will be produced. A cation with a greater standard electrode potential than a hydrogen ion will be reduced in its stead, and no hydrogen gas will be produced.

The following cations have lower electrode potential than H^+ and are therefore suitable for use as electrolyte cations: Li^+, Rb^+, K^+, Cs^+, Ba^{2+}, Sr^{2+}, Ca^{2+}, Na^+, and Mg^{2+}. Sodium and lithium are frequently used, as they form inexpensive, soluble salts.

If an acid is used as the electrolyte, the cation is H+, and there is no competitor for the H+ created by disassociating water. The most commonly used anion is sulfate (SO_4^{2-}), as it is very difficult to oxidize, with the standard potential for oxidation of this ion to the peroxodisulfate ion being -0.22 volts.

Strong acids such as sulfuric acid (H_2SO_4), and strong bases such as potassium hydroxide (KOH), and sodium hydroxide (NaOH) are frequently used as electrolytes.

A solid polymer electrolyte can also be used such as NAFION and when applied with a special catalyst on each side of the membrane can efficiently split the water molecule with as little as 1.8 Volts.

Techniques

Fundamental Demonstration

Two leads, running from the terminals of a battery, are placed in a cup of water with a quantity of electrolyte (not NaCl, anode creates chlorine gas) added to establish conductivity. Hydrogen and oxygen gases will stream from the oppositely charged electrode. Oxygen will collect at the anode and hydrogen will collect at the cathode.

Hofmann Voltameter

The Hofmann voltameter is often used as a small-scale electrolytic cell. It consists of three joined upright cylinders. The inner cylinder is open at the top to allow the addition of water and the electrolyte. A platinum electrode is placed at the bottom of each of the two side cylinders, connected to the positive and negative terminals of a source of electricity. When current is run through the Hofmann voltameter, gaseous oxygen forms at the anode and gaseous hydrogen at the cathode. Each gas displaces water and collects at the top of the two outer tubes, where it can be drawn off with a stopcock.

Industrial Electrolysis

Many industrial electrolysis cells are very similar to Hofmann voltameters, with complex platinum plates or honeycombs as electrodes. Generally the only time hydrogen is intentionally produced from electrolysis is for specific point of use application such as is the case with oxyhydrogen torches or when extremely high hydrogen purity or oxygen is desired. The vast majority of hydrogen is produced from hydrocarbons and as a result contains trace amounts of carbon monoxide among other impurities. The carbon monoxide impurity can be detrimental to various systems including many fuel cells.

High Pressure Electrolysis

High pressure electrolysis is the electrolysis of water with a compressed hydrogen output around 120-200 Bar (1740-2900 psi). By pressurising the hydrogen in the electrolyser the need for an external hydrogen compressor is eliminated, the average energy consumption for internal compression is around 3%.

High-temperature Electrolysis

High-temperature electrolysis (also HTE or steam electrolysis) is a method currently being investigated for water electrolysis with a heat engine. High temperature electrolysis is more efficient than traditional room-temperature electrolysis because some of the energy is supplied as heat, which is cheaper than electricity, and because the electrolysis reaction is more efficient at higher temperatures

Applications

About four percent of hydrogen gas produced worldwide is created by electrolysis. The majority of this hydrogen produced through electrolysis is a side product in the production of chlorine.

$$2\ NaCl + 2\ H_2O \rightarrow Cl_2 + H_2 + 2\ NaOH$$

The electrolysis of brine, a water sodium chloride mixture, is only half the electrolysis of water since the chloride ions are oxidized to chlorine rather than water being oxidized to oxygen. The hydrogen produced from this process is either burned, used for the production of specialty chemicals, or various other small scale applications.

The majority of hydrogen used industrially is derived from fossil fuels. One example is fossil fuel derived hydrogen used for the creation of ammonia for fertilizer via the Haber process and for converting heavy petroleum sources to lighter fractions via hydrocracking. The production of this hydrogen usually involves the formation of synthesis gas a mixture of H_2 and CO. Synthesis gas can be hydrogen enriched through the water gas shift reaction. In this reaction the carbon monoxide is reacted with water to produce more H_2 with CO_2 byproduct.

Efficiency

Water electrolysis does not convert 100% of the electrical energy into the chemical energy of hydrogen. The process requires more extreme potentials than what would be expected based on the cell's total reversible reduction potentials. This excess potential accounts for various forms of overpotential by which the extra energy is eventually lost as heat. For a well designed cell the largest overpotential is the reaction overpotential for the four electron oxidation of water to oxygen at the anode. An effective electrocatalyst to facilitate this reaction has not been developed. Platinum alloys are the default state of the art for this oxidation. The reverse reaction, the reduction of oxygen to water, is responsible for the greatest loss of efficiency in fuel cells. Developing a cheap effective electrocatalyst for this reaction would be a great advance

The simpler two-electron reaction to produce hydrogen at the cathode can be electrocatalyzed with almost no reaction overpotential by platinum or in theory a hydrogenase enzyme. If other, less effective, materials are used for the cathode then another large overpotential must be paid.

The energy efficiency of water electrolysis varies widely with the numbers cited below on the optimistic side. Some report 50-80% These values refer only to the efficiency of converting electrical energy into hydrogen's chemical energy. The energy lost in generating the electricity is not included. For instance, when considering a power plant that converts the heat of nuclear reactions into hydrogen via electrolysis, the total efficiency may be closer to 30-45 per cent.

11

Electrical Conduction

Electrical conduction is the movement of electrically charged particles through a transmission medium (electrical conductor). The movement of charge constitutes an electric current. The charge transport may result as a response to an electric field, or as a result of a concentration gradient in carrier density, that is, by diffusion . The physical parameters governing this transport depend upon the material.

Conduction in metals and resistors is well described by Ohm's Law, which states that the current is proportional to the applied electric field. The ease with which current density (current per unit area) j appears in a material is measured by the conductivity σ, defined as:

$$\mathbf{j} = \sigma \mathbf{E}$$

or its reciprocal resistivity ρ:

$$\mathbf{j} = \mathbf{E}/\rho$$

Conduction in semiconductor devices may occur by a combination of electric field (drift) and diffusion. The current density is then:

$$\mathbf{j} = \sigma \mathbf{E} + \mathbf{D}\, \nabla q n$$

with q the elementary charge and n the electron density. The carriers move in the direction of decreasing concentration, so for electrons a positive current results for a positive density gradient. If the carriers are holes, replace electron density n by the negative of the hole density p.

In linear anisotropic materials, ρ and D are tensors.

Electric currents in electrolytes are flows of electrically charged atoms (ions). For example, if an electric field is placed across a solution of Na^+ and Cl^-, the sodium ions will move constantly towards the negative electrode (cathode), while the chloride ions will move towards the positive electrode (anode). If the conditions are right, redox reactions will take place at the electrode surfaces, releasing electrons from the chloride, and allow electrons to be absorbed into the sodium.

Water-ice and certain solid electrolytes called proton conductors contain positive hydrogen ions which are free to move. In these materials, currents of electricity are composed of moving protons (as opposed to the moving electrons found in metals).

In certain electrolyte mixtures, populations of brightly-colored ions form the moving electric charges. The slow migration of these ions during an electric current is one example of a situation where a current is directly visible to human eyes.

Gases and Plasmas

In air, and other ordinary gases below the breakdown field, the dominant source of electrical conduction is via a relatively small number of mobile ions produced by radioactive gases, ultraviolet light, or cosmic rays. Since the electrical conductivity is extremely low, gases are dielectrics or insulators. However, once the applied electric field approaches the breakdown value, free electrons become sufficiently accelerated by the electric field to create additional free electrons by colliding, and ionizing, neutral gas atoms or molecules in a process called avalanche breakdown. The breakdown process forms a plasma that contains a significant number of mobile electrons and positive ions, causing it to behave as an electrical conductor. In the process, it forms a light emitting conductive path, such as a spark, arc or lightning.

Plasma is the state of matter where some of the electrons in a gas are stripped or "ionized" from their molecules or atoms. A plasma can be formed by high temperature, or by application of a high electric or alternating magnetic field as noted above. Due to their lower mass, the electrons in a plasma accelerate more quickly in response to an electric field than the heavier positive ions, and hence carry the bulk of the current.

Vacuum

Since a "perfect vacuum" contains no charged particles, vacuums normally behave as perfect insulators (they would be the greatest insulators known) However, metal electrode surfaces can cause a region of the vacuum to become conductive by injecting free electrons or ions through either field emission or thermionic emission. Thermionic emission occurs when the thermal energy exceeds the metal's work function, while field emission occurs when the electric field at the surface of the metal is high enough to cause tunneling, which results in the ejection of free electrons from the metal into the vacuum. Externally heated electrodes are often used to generate an electron cloud as in the filament or indirectly heated cathode of vacuum tubes. Cold electrodes can also spontaneously produce electron clouds via thermionic emission when small incandescent regions (called cathode spots or anode spots) are formed. These are incandescent regions of the electrode surface that are created by a localized high current flow. These regions may be initiated by field emission, but are then sustained by localized thermionic emission once a vacuum arc forms. These small electron-emitting regions can form quite rapidly, even explosively, on a metal surface subjected to a high electrical field. Vacuum tubes and sprytrons are some of the electronic switching and amplifying devices based on vacuum conductivity.

ELECTRIC CURRENT

Electric current is the flow of electric charge. The electric charge may be either electrons or ions.

The SI unit of electric current intensity is the ampere. Electric current is measured using an ammeter.

Current in a Metal Wire

A solid conductive metal contains a large population of mobile, or free, electrons. These electrons are bound to the metal lattice but not to any individual atom. Even with no external electric field applied, these electrons move about randomly due to thermal energy but, on average, there is zero net current within the metal. Given a plane through which the wire passes, the number of electrons moving from one side to the other in any period of time is on average equal to the number passing in the opposite direction. A typical wire for electrical conduction is the stranded copper wire.

When a metal wire is connected across the two terminals of a DC voltage source such as a battery, the source places an electric field across the conductor. The moment contact is made, the free electrons of the conductor are forced to drift toward the positive terminal under the influence of this field. The free electrons are therefore the current carrier in a typical solid conductor. For an electric current of 1 ampere, 1 coulomb of electric charge (which consists of about 6.242×10^{18} electrons) drifts every second through any plane through which the conductor passes.

For a steady flow, the current I in amperes can be calculated with the following equation:

$$I = \frac{Q}{t}$$

where

Q is the electric charge in coulombs transferred

t is the time in seconds

More generally, electric current can be represented as the time rate of change of charge, or

$$I = \frac{dQ}{dt}$$

Electric Currents in Other Media

In metallic solids, electricity flows by means of electrons, from lower to higher electrical potential. In other media, any stream of charged objects may constitute an electric current.

In a vacuum, a beam of ions or electrons may be formed. In other conductive materials, the electric current is due to the flow of both positively and negatively charged particles at the same time. In still others, the current is entirely due to positive charge flow. For example, the electric currents in electrolytes are flows of electrically charged atoms (ions), which exist in both positive and negative varieties. In a common lead-acid electrochemical cell, electric currents are composed of positive hydrogen ions (protons) flowing in one direction, and negative sulfate ions flowing in the other. Electric currents in sparks or plasma are flows of electrons as well as positive and negative ions. In ice and in certain solid electrolytes, the electric current is entirely composed of flowing ions. In a semiconductor it is sometimes useful think of the current as due to the flow of positive "holes" (the spots that should have an electron to make the conductor neutral). This is the case in a p-type semiconductor.

Current Density

Current density is a measure of the density of an electric current. It is defined as a vector whose magnitude is the electric current per cross-sectional area. In SI units, the current density is measured in amperes per square meter.

$$I = J.A$$

where I is current in the conductor, J is the current density, and A is the cross-sectional area. The dot product of two vector quantity signified that electric current is a scalar.

The Drift Speed of Electric Charges

The mobile charged particles within a conductor move constantly in random directions, like the particles of a gas. In order for there to be a net flow of charge, the particles must also move together with an average drift rate. Electrons are the charge carriers in metals and they follow an erratic path, bouncing from atom to atom, but generally drifting in the direction of the electric field. The speed at which they drift can be calculated from the equation:

$$I = nAvQ$$

where

I is the electric current

n is number of charged particles per unit volume

A is the cross-sectional area of the conductor

v is the drift velocity, and

Q is the charge on each particle.

Electric currents in solids typically flow very slowly. For example, in a copper wire of cross-section 0.5 mm^2, carrying a current of 5 A, the *drift velocity* of the electrons is of the order of a millimetre per second. To take a different example, in the near-vacuum inside a cathode ray tube, the electrons travel in near-straight lines ("ballistically") at about a tenth of the speed of light.

Any accelerating electric charge, and therefore any changing electric current, gives rise to an electromagnetic wave that propagates at very high speed outside the surface of the conductor. This speed is usually a significant fraction of the speed of light, as can be deduced from Maxwell's Equations, and is therefore many times faster than the drift velocity of the electrons. For example, in AC power lines, the waves of electromagnetic energy propagate through the space between the wires, moving from a source to a distant load, even though the electrons in the wires only move back and forth over a tiny distance.

The ratio of the speed of the electromagnetic wave to the speed of light in free space is called the velocity factor, and depends on the electromagnetic properties of the conductor and the insulating materials surrounding it, and on their shape and size.

The nature of these three velocities can be illustrated by an analogy with the three similar velocities associated with gases. The low drift velocity of charge carriers is analogous to air motion; in other words, winds. The high speed of electromagnetic waves is roughly analogous to the speed of sound in a gas; while the random motion of charges is analogous to heat - the thermal velocity of randomly vibrating gas particles.

Conventional Current

A flow of positive charge gives the same electric current as an opposite flow of negative charge. Thus, opposite flows of opposite charges contribute to a single electric current. For this reason, the polarity of the flowing charges can usually be ignored during measurements. All the flowing charges are assumed to have positive polarity, and this flow is called Conventional current. Conventional current represents the net effect of the current flow, without regard to the sign of the charge of the objects carrying the current.

In solid metals such as wires, the positive charge carriers are immobile, and only the negatively charged electrons flow. Because the electron carries negative charge, the electron motion in a metal is in the direction opposite to that of conventional (or electric) current.

Examples

Natural examples include lightning and the solar wind, the source of the polar auroras (the aurora borealis and aurora australis). The artificial form of electric current is the flow of conduction electrons in metal wires, such as the overhead power lines that deliver electrical energy across long distances and the smaller wires within electrical and electronic equipment. In electronics, other forms of electric current include the flow of electrons through resistors or through the vacuum in a vacuum tube, the flow of ions inside a battery or a neuron, and the flow of holes within a semiconductor. According to Ampère's law, an electric current produces a magnetic field.

Electromagnetism

Electric current produces a magnetic field. The magnetic field can be visualized as a pattern of circular field lines surrounding the wire. Electric current can be directly measured with a galvanometer, but this method involves breaking the circuit, which is sometimes inconvenient. Current can also be measured without breaking the circuit by detecting the magnetic field associated with the current. Devices used for this include Hall effect sensors, current clamps, current transformers, and Rogowski coils.

Reference Direction

When solving electrical circuits, the actual direction of current through a specific circuit element is usually unknown. Consequently, each circuit element is assigned a current variable with an arbitrarily chosen reference direction. When the circuit is solved, the circuit element currents may have positive or negative values. A negative value means that the actual direction of current through that circuit element is opposite that of the chosen reference direction.

Electrical Safety

The most obvious hazard is electrical shock, where a current passes through part of the body. It is the amount of current passing through the body that determines the effect, and this depends on the nature of the contact, the condition of the body part, the current path through the body and the voltage of the source. While a very small amount can cause a slight tingle, too much can cause severe burns if it passes through the skin or even cardiac arrest if enough passes through the heart. The effect also varies considerably from individual to individual. (For approximate figures see Shock Effects under electric shock.) Accidental electric heating can also be dangerous. An overloaded power cable is a frequent cause of fire. A battery as small as an AA cell placed in a pocket with metal coins can lead to a short circuit heating the battery and the coins which may inflict burns. NiCad, NiMh cells, and lithium batteries are particularly risky because they can deliver a very high current due to their low internal resistance.

12

Ions

An ion is an atom or molecule which has lost or gained one or more electrons, giving it a positive or negative electrical charge. According to the Model of Bohr this will be from or in the outer shield 'n'.

A negatively charged ion, which has more electrons than it has protons, is known as an **anion** *ana*: Greek 'up'). Conversely, a positively-charged ion, which has fewer electrons than protons, is known as a cation *kata*: Greek 'down') (pronounced *cat-eye-on*).

An ion consisting of a single atom is called a *monatomic ion*, but if it consists of two or more atoms, it is a *polyatomic ion*. Polyatomic ions containing oxygen, such as carbonate and sulfate, are called oxyanions. Polyatomic ions containing oxygen, such as carbonate and sulfate, are called oxyanions. When writing the chemical formula for an ion, its charge is written as a superscript "+" or "–" (depending on if the ion is positive + or negative –) following a number indicating the difference between the number of protons and the number of electrons. The number is omitted if it is equal to 1. For example, the sodium cation is written as Na^+, the "+"

indicating that it has one fewer electron than it has protons. The sulfate anion is written as SO_2^{-4} the "2−" indicating that it has *two* more electrons than it has protons. If an ion contains unpaired electrons, it is called a *radical* ion. Just like neutral radicals, radical ions are very positive.

Ions are denoted in the same way as electrically neutral atoms and molecules except for the presence of a superscript indicating the sign of the net electric charge and the number of electrons lost or gained, if more than one. For example: H^+ and SO_4^{2-}.

Formation

Formation of Monatomic ions

Monatomic ions are formed by the addition of electrons to the valence shall of the atom, which is the outer-most electron shell in an atom, or the losing of electrons from this shell. The inner shells of an atom are filled with electrons that are tightly bound to the positively charged atomic nucleus, and so do not participate in this kind of chemical interaction. The process of gaining or losing electrons from a neutral atom or molecule is called *ionization*.

Atoms can be ionized by bombardment with radiation, but the more usual process of ionization encountered in chemistry is the transfer of electrons between atoms or molecules. This transfer is usually driven by the attaining of stable ("closed shell") electronic configurations. Keep in mind that it takes an atom just as much energy to gain an electron as it takes to lose one. Therefore, atoms will gain or lose electrons depending on which action takes the least energy.

For example, a sodium atom, Na has a single electron in its valence shell, surrounding a stable, closed inner shell of 10 electrons. Since the 10-electron configuration is very stable, a sodium atom tends to lose its extra electron and attain this stable configuration, becoming a sodium *cation* in the process:

Na → Na^+ + e

On the other hand, a chlorine atom, Cl has 7 electrons in its valence shell, which is one short of the stable, filled shell with 8 electrons. Thus, a chlorine atom tends to *gain* an extra electron and attain a stable 8-electron configuration, becoming a chloride *anion* in the process:

Cl + e → Cl^-

This driving forces is what causes sodium and chlorine to undergo a chemical reaction, where the "extra" electron is transferred from sodium to chlorine, forming sodium cations and chloride anions. Being oppositely charged, these cations and anions form ionic bonds and combine together to form sodium chloride, NaCl, more commonly known as rock salt.

Na^+ + Cl^- → NaCl

Formation of Polyatomic and Molecular Ions

Polyatomic and molecular ions are often formed by the combination of elemental ions such as H^+ with neutral molecules or by the gain of such elemental ions from neutral molecules. A simple example of this is the ammonium ion NH_4^+ which can be formed by ammonia NH_3 accepting a proton, H^+. Ammonia and ammonium have the same number of electrons in essentially the same electronic configuration but differ in protons. The charge has been added by the addition of a proton (H^+) not the addition or removal of electrons. The distinction between this and the removal of an electron from the whole molecule is important in large systems because it usually results in much more stable ions with complete electron shells. For example $NH_3^{\cdot+}$ is not stable because of an incomplete valence shell around nitrogen and is in fact a radical ion.

Ionization Potential

The energy required to detach an electron in its lowest energy state from an atom or molecule of a gas with less net electric charge is called the *ionization potential*, or *ionization energy*. The *n*th ionization energy of an atom is the energy required to detach its *n*th electron after the first *n* - 1 electrons have already been detached.

Each successive ionization energy is markedly greater than the last. Particularly great increases occur after any given block of atomic orbitals is exhausted of electrons. For this reason, ions tend to form in ways that leave them with full orbital blocks. For example, sodium has one *valence electron*, in its outermost shell, so in ionized form it is commonly found with one lost electron, as Na^+. On the other side of the periodic table, chlorine has seven valence electrons, so in ionized form it is commonly found with one gained electron, as Cl^-. Francium has the lowest ionization energy of all the elements and fluorine has the greatest. The ionization energy of metals is generally much lower than the ionization energy of nonmetals, which is why metals will generally lose electrons to form positively-charged ions while nonmetals will generally gain electrons to form negatively-charged ions.

A neutral atom contains an equal number of Z protons in the nucleus and Z electrons in the electron shell. The electrons' negative charges thus exactly cancel the protons' positive charges. In the simple view of the Free electron model, a passing electron is therefore not attracted to a neutral atom and cannot bind to it. In reality, however, the atomic electrons form a cloud into which the additional electron penetrates, thus being exposed to a net positive charge part of the time. Furthermore, the additional charge displaces the original electrons and all of the Z + 1 electrons rearrange into a new configuration.

Ions

- **Anions** are negatively charged ions, formed when an atom gains electrons in a reaction. Anions are negatively charged because there are more electrons associated with them than there are protons in their nuclei.

- **Cations** are positively charged ions, formed when an atom loses electrons in a reaction, forming an '· electron hole'. Cations are the opposite of anions, since cations have fewer electrons than protons.
- **Radicals** or radical ions are atom groups that contain unpaired electrons and are highly reactive.

Plasma

A collection of non-aqueous gas-like ions, or even a gas containing a proportion of charged particles, is called a plasma, often called the *fourth state of matter* because its properties are quite different from solids, liquids, and gases. Astrophysical plasmas containing predominantly a mixture of electrons and protons, may make up as much as 99.9% of visible matter in the universe.

Applications

Ions are essential to life. Sodium, potassium, calcium and other ions play an important role in the cells of living organisms, particularly in cell membranes. They have many practical, everyday applications in items such as smoke detectors, and are also finding use in unconventional technologies such as ion engines. Inorganic dissolved ions are a component of total dissolved solids, an indicator of water quality in the world.

Voltage

Electrical tension (or voltage after its SI unit, the volt) is the difference of electrical potential between two points of an electrical or electronic circuit, expressed in volts It is the measurement of the potential for an electric field to cause an electric current in an electrical conductor. Voltage is a property of an electric field, not individual electrons. Voltage, as a definition, can more easily be described as a representation of the "carrier" of electrons. Depending on the difference of electrical potential it is called extra low voltage, low voltage, high voltage or extra high voltage. Specifically, voltage is equal to energy per unit charge.

Between two points in an electric field, such as exists in an electrical circuit, the difference in their electrical potentials is known as the electrical potential difference. This difference is proportional to the electrostatic force that tends to push electrons or other charge-carriers from one point to the other. Potential difference, electrical potential, and electromotive force are measured in volts, leading to the commonly used term voltage. Voltage is usually represented in equations by the symbols V, U, or E. (E is often preferred in academic writing, because it avoids the confusion between V and the SI symbol for the volt, which is also V.)

Electrical potential difference can be thought of as the ability to move electrical charge through a resistance. At a time in physics when the word force was used loosely, the potential difference was named the electromotive force or EMF—a term which is still used in certain contexts.

An electron moving across a voltage difference experiences a net change in energy, often measured in electron-volts. This effect is analogous to a mass falling through a given height difference in a gravitational field. When using the term 'potential difference' or voltage, one must be clear about the two points between which the voltage is specified or measured. There are two ways in which the term is used. This can lead to some confusion.

Voltage with Respect to a Common Point

One way in which the term voltage is used is when specifying the voltage of a point in a circuit. When this is done, it is understood that the voltage is usually being specified or measured with respect to a stable and unchanging point in the circuit that is known as ground or common. This voltage is really a voltage difference, one of the two points being the reference point, which is ground. A voltage can be positive or negative: "high" or "low" voltage may refer to the magnitude (the absolute value relative to the reference point). Thus, a large negative voltage can be described as a high voltage, although some writers do refer to negative voltages as "lower".

Voltage Between Two Stated Points

Another usage of the term "voltage" is in specifying how many volts are dropped across an electrical device (such as a resistor). In this case, the "voltage," or, more accurately, the "voltage drop across the device," is really the first voltage taken, relative to ground, on one terminal of the device minus a second voltage taken, relative to ground, on the other terminal of the device. In practice, the voltage drop across a device can be measured directly and safely using a voltmeter that is isolated from ground, provided that the maximum voltage capability of the voltmeter is not exceeded.

Two points in an electric circuit that are connected by an "ideal conductor," that is, a conductor without resistance and not within a changing magnetic field, have a potential difference of zero. However, other pairs of points may also have a potential difference of zero. If two such points are connected with a conductor, no current will flow through the connection.

Addition of Voltages

Voltage is additive in the following sense: the voltage between A and C is the sum of the voltage between A and B and the voltage between B and C. The various voltages in a circuit can be computed using Kirchhoff's circuit laws.

When talking about alternating current (AC) there is a difference between instantaneous voltage and average voltage. Instantaneous voltages can be added as for direct current (DC), but average voltages can be meaningfully added only when they apply to signals that all have the same frequency and phase.

Hydraulic Analogy

If one imagines water circulating in a network of pipes, driven by pumps in the absence of gravity, as an analogy of an electrical circuit, then the potential difference corresponds to the fluid pressure difference between two points. If there is a pressure difference between two points, then water flowing from the first point to the second will be able to do work, such as driving a turbine.

This hydraulic analogy is a useful method of teaching a range of electrical concepts. In a hydraulic system, the work done to move water is equal to the pressure multiplied by the volume of water moved. Similarly, in an electrical circuit, the work done to move electrons or other charge-carriers is equal to 'electrical pressure' (an old term for voltage) multiplied by the quantity of electrical charge moved. Voltage is a convenient way of quantifying the ability to do work. In relation to electric current, the larger the gradient (voltage or hydraulic) the greater the current (assuming resistance is constant).

13

Galvanic Cell

The Galvanic cell, named after Luigi Galvani, is a part of a battery consisting of an electrochemical cell with two different metals connected by a salt bridge or a porous disk between the individual half-cells. It is sometimes called a Voltaic cell.

Common usage of the word "battery" has evolved to include a single Galvanic cell, but the first batteries had many Galvanic cells. The Galvanic cell should not be confused with the electrolytic cell.

History

In 1780, Luigi Galvani discovered that when two different metals (copper and zinc for example) were connected together and then both touched to different parts of a nerve of a frog leg at the same time, they made the leg contractHe called this "animal electricity". The Voltaic pile invented by Alessandro Volta in the 1800s is similar to the galvanic cell. These discoveries paved the way for electrical batteries.

Description

A galvanic cell consists of two half-cells. Each half-cell has:

1. an electrode, which in the figure are the plates of Zn (zinc) and Cu (copper); and
2. an electrolyte, which in the figure are aqueous solutions of $ZnSO_4$ and $CuSO_4$.

The metal of a metallic electrode tends to go into solution, thereby releasing positively charged metal ions into the electrolyte, and retaining negatively charged electrons on the electrode. Thus each half-cell has its own half-reaction. For the Daniell cell, depicted in the figure, the Zn atoms have a greater tendency to go into solution than do the Cu atoms. More precisely, the electrons on the Zn electrode have a higher energy than the electrons on the Cu electrode. Because the electrons have negative charge, to give electrons on it a higher energy the Zn electrode must have a more negative electrical potential than the Cu electrode. However, in the absence of an external connection between the electrodes, no current can flow.

When the electrodes are connected externally (as in the figure, with wire and a voltmeter), the electrons tend to flow from the more negative electrode (Zn) to the more positive electrode (Cu). Because the electrons have negative charge, this produces an electric current that is opposite the electron flow. At the same time, an equal ionic current flows through the electrolyte. For every two electrons that flow from the Zn electrode through the external connection to the Cu electrode, on the electrolyte side a Zn atom must go into solution as a Zn^{2+} ion, at the same time replacing the two electrons that have left the Zn electrode by the external connection. By definition, the anode is the electrode where oxidation (removal of electrons) takes place, so in this galvanic cell the Zn electrode is the anode. Because the Cu has gained two electrons from the external connection, it must release two electrons at the electrolyte side, where a Cu^{2+} ion, from the Copper Sulfate, plates onto the Cu electrode. By definition, the cathode is the electrode where reduction (gain of electrons) takes place, so the Cu electrode is the cathode. Electrons will flow from the Anode to the Cathode.

An essential piece of a Galvanic Cell is the salt bridge. The salt bridge serves the vital role of allowing each half-cell's charge to be balanced while preventing the solutions from mixing with each other. Should the solutions be mixed, the reaction will be purely chemical and will not require electrons to flow through the wire — thus, no electricity can be harbored from the cell. Should the charges not be balanced, the anode will have an abundance of positive ions, and the cathode will have an abundance of negative ions. Electrons will not flow with this imbalance. The salt in the salt bridge, however, will ionize and neutralize the charges in each half-cell, allowing the reaction to proceed.

Notation

The galvanic cells, as the one shown in the figure, are conventionally described using the following notation:

$Zn_{(s)}$ | $ZnSO_{4(aq)}$ || $CuSO_{4(aq)}$ | $Cu_{(s)}$

(anode) (cathode)

An alternate notation for this cell would be:

$Zn_{(s)}$ | $Zn^{+2}_{(aq)}$ || $Cu^{+2}_{(aq)}$ | $Cu_{(s)}$

where: (s) denotes solid; (aq) means aqueous solution; the vertical bar, |, denotes a phase boundary; and the double vertical bar, ||, denotes a liquid junction for which the junction potential is near zero, such as a salt bridge.

Corrosion

In this way the anode is consumed or corroded. When the anode material corrodes entirely away, the cell's potential drops and the current halts. The metal may be regarded as the fuel that powers the device. A similar process is used in electroplating. The ionic current in the electrolyte is equal to the current in the external circuit, so a complete circuit is formed with a path through the electrolyte.

As can be seen, electrons flow from the oxidized ion at the anode to the reduced atom (formerly an ion) at the cathode. The flow due to this redox reaction constitutes the current.

Electric Potential

The potential of a cell can be determined by use of a standard potential table for the two half cells involved. An oxidation potential table could also be used, but the reduction table is more common. The calculation assumes that the cell operates at zero current flowing through the circuit.

The first step is to identify the two metals reacting in the cell. Then one looks up the E^o (standard electrode potential, in volts) for each of the two half reactions. The electric potential for the cell is equal to the more positive E^o value minus the more negative E^o value.

For example, in the picture above the solutions are $CuSO_4$ and $ZnSO_4$. Each solution has a corresponding metal strip in it, and a salt bridge or porous disk connecting the two solutions and allowing SO_4^{2-} ions to flow freely between the copper and zinc solutions. In order to calculate the electric potential one looks up copper and zinc's half reactions and finds that:

$Cu^{2+} + 2^{e-} \rightarrow Cu$ (E = +0.34 V);

$Zn^{2+} + 2^{e-} \rightarrow Zn$ (E = -0.76 V)

Thus the overall reaction that is going on is

$Cu^{2+} + Zn \rightarrow Cu + Zn^{2+}$

The electric potential is then +0.34 V - -0.76 V = 1.10 V under standard conditions and when no current flows in the cell.

If the cell is operated under non-standard conditions, the potentials must be adapted using the Nernst equation. If a current is allowed to flow in the circuit, the potential is going to shift towards zero in comparison with that predicted by the Nernst equation.

When measurements of the cell potential are performed, then the positive terminal of the electrometer needs to be be connected to the right-hand half-cell. This is because the potential of the cell is defined as:

$$E_{Cell} = E_{Right} - E_{Left}$$

Galvanic Corrosion

Galvanic corrosion is a process that degrades metals electrochemically. This corrosion occurs when two dissimilar metals are placed in contact with each other in the presence of an electrolyte, such as salt water, forming a galvanic cell. A cell can also be formed if the same metal is exposed to two different concentrations of electrolyte. The resulting electrochemical potential then develops an electric current that electrolytically dissolves the less noble material.

Electrolytic Cell

An electrolytic cell decomposes chemical compounds by means of electrical energy, in a process called electrolysis; the Greek word lysis means to break up. The result is that the chemical energy is increased. Important examples of electrolysis are the decomposition of water into hydrogen and hydroxide, and bauxite into aluminium and other chemicals.

Components

An electrolytic cell has three component parts: an electrolyte and two electrodes (a cathode and an anode). The electrolyte is usually a solution of water or other solvents in which ions are dissolved. Molten salts such as sodium chloride are also electrolytes. When driven by an external voltage applied to the electrodes, the electrolyte provides ions that flow to and from the electrodes, where charge-transferring, or faradaic, or redox, reactions can take place. Only for an external electrical potential (i.e. voltage) of the correct polarity and large enough magnitude can an electrolytic cell decompose a normally stable, or inert chemical compound in the solution. The electrical energy provided undoes the effect of spontaneous chemical reactions.

Galvanic Cells Compared to Electrolytic Cells

In contrast, a battery or Galvanic cell, converts chemical energy into electrical energy, by using spontaneous chemical reactions that take place at the electrodes. Each galvanic cell has its own characteristic voltage (defined as the energy release per electron transfer from one electrode to the other). A simple galvanic cell will consist only of an electrolyte and two different electrodes. (Galvanic cells can also be made by connecting two half-cells, each with its own electrode and electrolyte, by an ion-transporting "bridge", usually a salt bridge; these cells are more complex.) The electrodes typically are two metals, which naturally have different reaction potentials relative to the electrolyte. This causes ions of one of the electrodes to preferentially enter the solution at one electrode, and another ion to leave the solution at the other electrode. This generates an electric current across the electrolyte, which will drive electric current through a wire that makes an exterior connection to each of the electrodes. A galvanic cell uses electrodes of different metals, whereas an electrolytic cell may use the same metal for cathode and anode.

A rechargeable battery, such as a AA NiMH cell or a single cell of a lead-acid battery, acts as a galvanic cell when discharging (converting chemical energy to electrical energy), and an electrolytic cell when being charged (converting electrical energy to chemical energy).

Anode and Cathode Definitions Depend on Charge and Discharge

Michael Faraday defined the cathode as the electrode to which cations flow (positively charged ions, like silver ions Ag^{+}), to be reduced by reacting with (negatively-charged) electrons on the cathode. Likewise he defined the anode as the electrode to which anions flow (negatively charged ions, like chloride ions Cl^{-}), to be oxidized by depositing electrons on the anode. Thus positive electric current flows from the cathode to the anode. To an external wire connected to the electrodes of a battery, thus forming an electric circuit, the cathode is positive and the anode is negative.

Consider two voltaic cells, A and B, with the voltage of A greater than the voltage of B. Mark the positive and negative electrodes as anode and cathode. Place them in a circuit with anode near anode and cathode near cathode, so the cells will tend to drive current in opposite directions. The cell with the larger voltage discharges, making it a voltaic cell. Likewise the cell with the smaller voltage charges, making it an electrolytic cell. For the electrolytic cell, the external markings of anode and cathode are opposite the chemical definition. That is, the electrode marked as anode for discharge acts as the cathode while charging and the electrode marked as cathode acts as the anode while charging.

Uses

As already noted, water, particularly when ions are added (salt water or acidic water) can be *electrolyzed* (subject to electrolysis). When driven by an external source of voltage, H^+ ions flow to the cathode to combine with electrons to produce hydrogen gas in a reduction reaction. Likewise, OH^- ions flow to the anode to release electrons and an H^+ ion to produce oxygen gas in an oxidation reaction.

In molten sodium chloride, when a current is passed through the salt the anode oxidizes chloride ions (Cl^-) to chlorine gas, releasing electrons to the anode. Likewise the cathode reduces sodium ions (Na^+), which accept electrons from the cathode and deposits on the cathode as sodium metal.

NaCl dissolved in water can also be electrolyzed. The anode oxidixes chloride ions (Cl^-), and Cl_2 gas is still produced. However, at the cathode, instead of sodium ions being reduced to sodium metal, water molecules are reduced to hydroxide ions (OH^-) and hydrogen gas (H_2). The overall result of the electrolysis is the production of chlorine gas and aqueous sodium hydroxide (NaOH) solution.

Commercially, electrolytic cells are used in electrorefining and electrowinning of several non-ferrous metals. Almost all high-purity aluminium, copper, zinc and lead is produced industrially in electrolytic cells.

14

Battery (Electricity)

In electronics, a battery or voltaic cell is a combination of one or more electrochemical Galvanic cells which store chemical energy that can be converted into electric potential energy, creating electricity. Since the invention of the first Voltaic pile in 1800 by Alessandro Volta, the battery has become a common power source for many household and industrial applications, and is now a multi-billion dollar industry.

The name "battery" was coined by Benjamin Franklin for an arrangement of multiple Leyden jars (an early type of capacitor) after a battery of cannon Common usage includes a single electrical cell in the definition.

History

An early form of electrochemical battery called the Baghdad Battery may have been used in antiquity.However, the modern development of batteries started with the Voltaic pile, invented by the Italian physicist Alessandro Volta in 1800.

In 1791, Luigi Galvani published a report on "animal electricity."He created an electric circuit consisting of two different metals, with one touching a frog's leg and the other touching both the leg and the first metal, thus closing the circuit. In modern terms, the frog's leg served as both the electrolyte and the sensor, and the metals served as electrodes. He noticed that even though the frog was dead, its legs would twitch when he touched them with the metals.

Within a year, Volta realized the frog's moist tissues could be replaced by cardboard soaked in salt water, and the frog's muscular response could be replaced by another form of electrical detection. He already had studied the electrostatic phenomenon of capacitance, which required measurements of electric charge and of electrical potential ("tension"). Building on this experience, Volta was able to detect electric current through his system, also called a Galvanic cell. The terminal voltage of a cell that is not discharging is called its electromotive force (emf), and has the same unit as electrical potential, named (voltage) and measured in volts, in honour of Volta. In 1800, Volta invented the battery by placing many voltaic cells in series, literally piling them one above the other. This Voltaic pile gave a greatly enhanced net emf for the combination, with a voltage of about 50 volts for a 32-cell pile *n* many parts of Europe batteries continue to be called piles.

Volta did not appreciate that the voltage was due to chemical reactions. He thought that his cells were an inexhaustible source of energy and that the associated chemical effects (e.g. corrosion) were a mere nuisance, rather than an unavoidable consequence of their operation, as Michael Faraday showed in 1834. According to Faraday, cations (positively charged ions) are attracted to the cathode, and anions (negatively charged ions) are attracted to the anode.

Although early batteries were of great value for experimental purposes, in practice their voltages fluctuated and they could not provide a large current for a sustained period. Later, starting with the Daniell cell in 1836, batteries provided more reliable currents and were adopted by industry for use in stationary devices, particularly in telegraph networks where they were the only practical source of electricity, since electrical distribution networks did not then exist These wet cells used liquid electrolytes, which were prone to leakage and spillage if not handled correctly. Many used glass jars to hold their components, which made them fragile. These characteristics made wet cells unsuitable for portable appliances. Near the end of the nineteenth century, the invention of dry cell batteries, which replaced the liquid electrolyte with a paste, made portable electrical devices practical.

Since then, batteries have gained popularity as they became portable and useful for a variety of purposes According to a 2005 estimate, the worldwide battery industry generates US$48 billion in sales each year with 6% annual growth.

How Batteries Work

A battery is a device that converts chemical energy directly to electrical energy It consists of one or more voltaic cells. Each voltaic cell consists of two half cells connected in series by a conductive electrolyte containing anions and cations. One half-cell includes electrolyte and the electrode to which anions (negatively-charged ions) migrate, i.e. the anode or negative electrode; the other half-cell includes electrolyte and the electrode to which cations (positively-charged ions) migrate, i.e. the cathode or positive electrode. In the redox reaction that powers the battery, reduction (addition of electrons) occurs to cations at the cathode, while oxidation (removal of electrons) occurs to anions at the anode. The electrodes do not touch each other but are electrically connected by the electrolyte, which can be either solid or liquid Many cells use two half-cells with different electrolytes. In that case each half-cell is enclosed in a container, and a separator that is porous to ions but not the bulk of the electrolytes prevents mixing.

Each half cell has an electromotive force (or emf), determined by its ability to drive electric current from the interior to the exterior of the cell. The net emf of the battery is the difference between the emfs of its half-cells, as first recognized by Volta Thus, if the electrodes have emfs ε_1 and ε_2 then the net emf is ε_1-ε_2 in other words, the net emf is difference between the reduction potentials of the half-reactions

The electrical potential difference, or ΔV_{bat} across the terminals of a battery is known as terminal voltage and is measured in volts. The terminal voltage of a battery that is neither charging nor discharging is called the open-circuit voltage and equals the emf of the battery. Because of internal resistance the terminal voltage of a battery that is discharging is smaller in magnitude than the open-circuit voltage and the terminal voltage of a battery that is charging exceeds the open-circuit voltage An ideal battery has negligible internal resistance, so it would maintain a constant terminal voltage of ε until exhausted, then dropping to zero. If such a battery maintained 1.5 volts and stored a charge of one Coulomb then on complete discharge it would perform 1.5 Joule of work In actual batteries, the internal resistance increases under discharge and the open circuit voltage also decreases under discharge. If the voltage and resistance are plotted against time, the resulting graphs typically are a curve; the shape of the curve varies according to the chemistry and internal arrangement employed.

As stated above, the voltage developed across a cell's terminals depends on the energy release of the chemical reactions of its electrodes and electrolyte. Alkaline and carbon-zinc cells have different chemistries but approximately the same emf of 1.5 volts; likewise NiCd and NiMH cells have different chemistries, but approximately the same emf of 1.2 volts On the other hand the high electrochemical potential changes in the reactions of lithium compounds give lithium cells emfs of 3 volts or more.

Types of Batteries

From top to bottom: Two button cells, a 9-volt PP3 battery, an AAA cell, an AA cell, a C cell, a D Cell, a large 3R12.There are many general types of electrochemical cells, including galvanic cells, electrolytic cells, fuel cells, flow cells and voltaic piles. A battery's characteristics may vary due to many factors including internal chemistry, current drain and temperature.

Batteries are classified into two broad categories, each type with advantages and disadvantages.

Primary batteries irreversibly (within limits of practicality) transform chemical energy to electrical energy. When the initial supply of reactants is exhausted, energy cannot be readily restored to the battery by electrical means.

Secondary batteries can be recharged; that is, they can have their chemical reactions reversed by supplying electrical energy to the cell, restoring their original composition.

Historically, some types of primary batteries used, for example, for telegraph circuits, were restored to operation by replacing the components of the battery consumed by the chemical reaction. Secondary batteries are not indefinitely rechargeable due to dissipation of the active materials, loss of electrolyte and internal corrosion.

Primary Batteries

Primary batteries can produce current immediately on assembly. Disposable batteries, also called primary cells, are intended to be used once and discarded. These are most commonly used in portable devices that have low current drain, are only used intermittently, or are used well away from an alternative power source, such as in alarm and communication circuits where other electric power is only intermittently available. Disposable primary cells cannot be reliably recharged, since the chemical reactions are not easily reversible and active materials may not return to their original forms. Battery manufacturers recommend against attempting to recharge primary cells.

Common types of disposable batteries include zinc-carbon batteries and alkaline batteries. Generally, these have higher energy densities than rechargeable batteries but disposable batteries do not fare well under high-drain applications with loads under 75 ohms (75 O).

Secondary Batteries

Secondary batteries must be charged before use; they are usually assembled with active materials in the discharged state. Rechargeable batteries or secondary cells can be recharged by applying electrical current, which reverses the chemical reactions that occur during its use. Devices to supply the appropriate current are called chargers or rechargers.

The oldest form of rechargeable battery is the lead-acid battery, a type of wet cell. This battery is notable in that it contains a liquid in an unsealed container, requiring that the battery be kept upright and the area be well ventilated to ensure safe dispersal of the hydrogen gas produced by these batteries during overcharging. The lead-acid battery is also very heavy for the amount of electrical energy it can supply. Despite this, its low manufacturing cost and its high surge current levels make its use common where a large capacity (over approximately 10Ah) is required or where the weight and ease of handling are not concerns.

A common form of the lead-acid battery is the modern car battery, which can generally deliver a peak current of 450 amperesAn improved type of liquid electrolyte battery is the sealed valve regulated lead acid (VRLA) battery, popular in the automotive industry as a replacement for the lead-acid wet cell. The VRLA battery uses an immobilized sulfuric acid electrolyte, reducing the chance of leakage and extending shelf life. VRLA batteries have the electrolyte immobilized, usually by one of two means:

- Gel batteries (or "gel cell") contain a semi-solid electrolyte to prevent spillage.
- Absorbed Glass Mat (AGM) batteries absorb the electrolyte in a special fiberglass matting.

Other portable rechargeable batteries include several "dry cell" types, which are sealed units and are therefore useful in appliances such as mobile phones and laptop computers. Cells of this type (in order of increasing power density and cost) include nickel-cadmium (NiCd), nickel metal hydride (NiMH) and lithium-ion (Li-ion) cells. By far, Li-ion has the highest share of the dry cell rechargeable market. Meanwhile, NiMH has replaced NiCd in most applications due to its higher capacity, but NiCd remains in use in power tools, two-way radios, and medical equipment.

Recent developments include batteries with embedded functionality such as USBCELL, with a built-in charger and USB connector within the AA format, enabling the battery to be charged by plugging into a USB port without a charger and low self-discharge (LSD) mix chemistries such as Hybrio, ReCyko, and Eneloop where cells are precharged prior to shipping.

Battery Capacity and Discharging

The more electrolyte and electrode material there is in the cell, the greater the capacity of the cell. Thus a small cell has less capacity than a larger cell, given the same chemistry (e.g. alkaline cells), though they develop the same open-circuit voltage.

Because of the chemical reactions within the cells, the capacity of a battery depends on the discharge conditions such as the magnitude of the current, the duration of the current, the allowable terminal voltage of the battery, temperature and other factors The available capacity of a battery depends upon the rate at which it is discharged. If a battery is discharged at a relatively high rate, the available capacity will be lower than expected.

The battery capacity that battery manufacturers print on a battery is the product of 20 hours multiplied by the maximum constant current that a new battery can supply for 20 hours at 68° F (20° C), down to a predetermined terminal voltage per cell. A battery rated at 100 A · h will deliver 5 A over a 20 hour period at room temperature. However, if it is instead discharged at 50 A, it will run out of charge before the 2 hours as theoretically expected.

For this reason, a battery capacity rating is always related to an expected discharge duration.

$$t = \frac{Q}{I}$$

where

Q is the battery capacity (typically given in mA·h or A·h).

I is the current drawn from battery (mA or A).

t is the amount of time (in hours) that a battery can sustain.

The relationship between current, discharge time, and capacity for a lead acid battery is expressed by Peukert's law. Theoretically, a battery should provide the same amount of energy regardless of the discharge rate, but in real batteries, internal energy losses cause the efficiency of a battery to vary at different discharge rates. When discharging at low rate, the battery's energy is delivered more efficiently than at higher discharge rates.

In general, the higher the ampere-hour rating, the longer the battery will last for a certain load. Installing batteries with different A·h ratings will not affect the operation of a device rated for a specific voltage unless the load limits of the battery are exceeded. Theoretically, a battery would operate at its A·h rating, but realistically, high-drain loads like digital cameras can result in lower actual energy, most notably for alkaline batteries.For example, a battery rated at 2000 mA·h may not sustain a current of 1 A for the full two hours.

Battery Lifetime

Even if never taken out of the original package, disposable (or "primary") batteries can lose 8 to 20 percent of their original charge every year at a temperature of about 20°–30°C. This is known as the "self discharge" rate and is due to non-current-producing "side" chemical reactions, which occur within the cell even if no load is applied to it. The rate of the side reactions is reduced if the batteries are stored at low temperature, although some batteries can be damaged by freezing. High or low temperatures may reduce battery performance. This will affect the initial voltage of the battery. For an AA alkaline battery this initial volte is approximately normally distributed around 1.6 volts.

Life of Rechargeable Batteries

Rechargeable batteries traditionally self-discharge more rapidly than disposable alkaline batteries, especially nickel-based batteries; a freshly charged NiCd loses 10% of its charge in the first 24 hours, and thereafter discharges at a rate of about 10% a month. However, modern lithium designs have reduced the self-discharge rate to a relatively low level (but still poorer than for primary batteries). Most nickel-based batteries are partially discharged when purchased, and must be charged before first use.

Although rechargeable batteries may be refreshed by charging, they still suffer degradation through usage. Low-capacity nickel metal hydride (NiMH) batteries (1700-2000 mA·h) can be charged for about 1000 cycles, whereas high capacity NiMH batteries (above 2500 mA·h) can be charged for about 500 cyclesNickel cadmium (NiCd) batteries tend to be rated for 1,000 cycles before their internal resistance increases beyond usable values. Normally a fast charge, rather than a slow overnight charge, will result in a shorter battery lifespan However, if the overnight charger is not "smart" and cannot detect when the battery is fully charged, then overcharging is likely, which will damage the battery Degradation usually occurs because electrolyte migrates away from the electrodes or because active material falls off the electrodes. NiCd batteries suffer the drawback that they should be fully discharged before recharge. Without full discharge, crystals may build up on the electrodes, thus decreasing the active surface area and increasing internal resistance. This decreases battery capacity and causes the dreaded "memory effect". These electrode crystals can also penetrate the electrolyte separator, thereby causing shorts. NiMH, although similar in chemistry, does not suffer from "memory effect" to quite this extent When a battery reaches the end of its lifetime, it will not suddenly lose all of its capacity; rather, its capacity will gradually decrease.

Automotive lead-acid rechargeable batteries have a much harder life Because of vibration, shock, heat, cold, and sulfation of their lead plates, few automotive batteries last beyond six years of regular use Automotive starting batteries have many thin plates to provide as much current as possible in a reasonably small package. In general, the thicker the plates, the longer the life of the battery Typically they are only drained a small amount before recharge. Care should be taken to avoid deep discharging a starting battery, since each charge and discharge cycle causes active material to be shed from the plates.

"Deep-cycle" lead-acid batteries such as those used in electric golf carts have much thicker plates to aid their longevity. The main benefit of the lead-acid battery is its low cost; the main drawbacks are its large size and weight for a given capacity and voltage Lead-acid batteries should never be discharged to below 20% of their full capacity, because internal resistance will cause heat and damage when they are recharged. Deep-cycle lead-acid systems often use a low-charge warning light or a low-charge power cut-off switch to prevent the type of damage that will shorten the battery's life

Extending Battery Life

Battery life can be extended by storing the batteries at a low temperature, as in a refrigerator or freezer, because the chemical reactions in the batteries are slower. Such storage can extend the life of alkaline batteries by ~5%; while the charge of rechargeable batteries can be extended from a few days up to several months In order to reach their maximum voltage, batteries must be returned to room temperature; discharging an alkaline battery at 250 mAH at 0°C is only half as efficient as it is at 20°C As a result, alkaline battery manufacturers like Duracell do not recommend refrigerating or freezing batteries

Hazards

Explosion

A battery explosion is caused by the misuse or malfunction of a battery, such as attempting to recharge a primary (non-rechargeable) battery or short circuiting a battery With car batteries, explosions are most likely to occur when a short circuit generates very large currents. In addition, car batteries liberate hydrogen when they are overcharged (because of electrolysis of the water in the electrolyte). Normally the amount of overcharging is very small, as is the amount of explosive gas developed, and the gas dissipates quickly. However, when "jumping" a car battery, the high current can cause the rapid release of large volumes of hydrogen, which can be ignited by a nearby spark (for example, when removing the jumper cables).

When a battery is recharged at an excessive rate, an explosive gas mixture of hydrogen and oxygen may be produced faster than it can escape from within the walls of the battery, leading to pressure build-up and the possibility of the battery case bursting. In extreme cases, the battery acid may spray violently from the casing of the battery and cause injury. Overcharging—that is, attempting to charge a battery beyond its electrical capacity—can also lead to a battery explosion, leakage, or irreversible damage to the battery. It may also cause damage to the charger or device in which the overcharged battery is later used. Additionally, disposing of a battery in fire may cause an explosion as steam builds up within the sealed case of the battery

Environmental Concerns

The widespread use of batteries has created many environmental concerns, such as toxic metal pollution Battery manufacture consumes resources and often involves hazardous chemicals. Used batteries also contribute to electronic waste. Some areas now have battery recycling services available to recover some of the materials from used batteries. Batteries may be harmful or fatal if swallowed. Recycling or proper disposal prevents dangerous elements (such as lead, mercury, and cadmium) found in some types of batteries from entering the environment. In the United States, Americans purchase nearly three billion batteries annually, and about 179,000 tons of those end up in landfills across the country.

In the United States, the Mercury-Containing and Rechargeable Battery Management Act of 1996 banned the sale of mercury-containing batteries (except small button cell batteries), enacted uniform labeling requirements for rechargeable batteries, and required that rechargeable batteries be easily removable California, and New York City prohibit the disposal of rechargeable batteries in solid waste, and along with Maine require recycling of cell phones The rechargeable battery industry has nationwide recycling programs in the United States and Canada, with dropoff points at local retailers.

The Battery Directive of the European Union has similar requirements, in addition to requiring increased recycling of batteries, and promoting research on improved battery recycling methods.

15

Organic Redox Reaction

Redox (shorthand for reduction-oxidation reaction) describes all chemical reactions in which atoms have their oxidation number (oxidation state) changed. This can be either a simple redox process such as the oxidation of carbon to yield carbon dioxide or the reduction of carbon by hydrogen to yield methane (CH_4), or it can be a complex process such as the oxidation of sugar in the human body through a series of very complex electron transfer processes.

The term redox comes from the two concepts of reduction and oxidation. It can be explained in simple terms:

Oxidation describes the loss of electrons/hydrogen or gain of oxygen/increase in oxidation state by a molecule, atom or ion.

Reduction describes the gain of electrons/hydrogen or a loss of oxygen/decrease in oxidation state by a molecule, atom or ion.

Though sufficient for many purposes, these descriptions are not precisely correct. Oxidation and reduction properly refer to a change in oxidation number — the actual transfer of electrons may never occur. Thus, oxidation is better defined as an increase in oxidation number, and reduction as a decrease in oxidation number. In practice, the transfer of electrons will always cause a change in oxidation number, but there are many reactions that are classed as "redox" even though no electron transfer occurs (such as those involving covalent bonds).

Non-redox reactions, which do not involve changes in formal charge, are known as metathesis reactions.

Oxidizing and Reducing Agents

Substances that have the ability to oxidize other substances are said to be oxidative and are known as oxidizing agents, oxidants, or oxidizers. Put another way, the oxidant removes electrons from another substance, and is, thus, reduced itself. And, because it "accepts" electrons, it is also called an electron acceptor.

Oxidants are usually chemical substances with elements in high oxidation numbers (e.g., H_2O_2, MnO_4^-, CrO_3, $Cr_2O_7^{2-}$, OsO_4) or highly electronegative substances that can gain one or two extra electrons by oxidizing a substance (O, F, Cl, Br).

Substances that have the ability to reduce other substances are said to be reductive and are known as reducing agents, reductants, or reducers. Put in another way, the reductant transfers electrons to another substance, and is, thus, oxidized itself. And, because it "donates" electrons it is also called an electron donor. Reductants in chemistry are very diverse. *Metal reduction*—electropositive elemental metals can be used (Li, Na, Mg, Fe, Zn, Al). These metals donate or *give away* electrons readily. Reactions-Reducing Agents Other kinds of reductants are *hydride transfer reagents* ($NaBH_4$, $LiAlH_4$), these reagents are widely used in organic chemistry primarily in the reduction of carbonyl compounds to alcohols. Another useful method is reductions involving hydrogen gas (H_2) with a palladium, platinum, or nickel catalyst. These *catalytic reductions* are primarily used in the reduction of carbon-carbon double or triple bonds.

The chemical way to look at redox processes is that the reductant transfers electrons to the oxidant. Thus, in the reaction, the reductant or *reducing agent* loses electrons and is oxidized, and the oxidant or *oxidizing agent* gains electrons and is reduced. The pair of an oxidizing and reducing agent that are involved in a particular reaction is called a redox pair.

Examples of Redox Reactions

A good example is the reaction between hydrogen and fluorine:

$$H_2 + F_2 \rightarrow 2HF$$

We can write this overall reaction as two half-reactions: the oxidation reaction

$$H_2 \rightarrow 2H^+ + 2e^-$$

and the reduction reaction:

$$F_2 + 2e^- \rightarrow 2F^-$$

Analyzing each half-reaction in isolation can often make the overall chemical process clearer. Because there is no net change in charge during a redox reaction, the number of electrons in excess in the oxidation reaction must equal the number consumed by the reduction reaction.

Elements, even in molecular form, always have an oxidation number of zero. In the first half-reaction, hydrogen is oxidized from an oxidation number of zero to an oxidation number of +1. In the second half-reaction, fluorine is reduced from an oxidation number of zero to an oxidation number of -1.

When adding the reactions together the electrons cancel:

$$H_2 \rightarrow 2H^+ + 2e^-$$

$$F_2 + 2e^- \rightarrow 2F^-$$

$$\overline{H_2 + F_2 \rightarrow 2H^+ + 2F^-}$$

And the ions combine to form hydrogen fluoride:

$H_2 + F_2 \rightarrow 2H^+ + 2F^- \rightarrow 2HF$

Displacement Reactions

Redox occurs in single displacement reactions or substitution reactions. The redox component of these types of reactions is the change of oxidation state (charge) on certain atoms, not the actual exchange of atoms in the compounds.

For example, in the reaction between iron and copper(II) sulphate solution:

$Fe + CuSI_4 \rightarrow FeSO_4 + Cu$

The ionic equation for this reaction is:

$Fe + Cu^{2+} \rightarrow Fe^{2+} + Cu$

As two half-equations, it is seen that the iron is oxidized:

$Fe \rightarrow Fe^{2+} + 2^{e-}$

And the copper is reduced:

$Cu^{2+} + 2e^- \rightarrow Cu$

Other examples

iron(II) oxidizes to iron(III):

$Fe^{2+} + Fe^{3+} + e^-$

hydrogen peroxide reduces to hydroxide in the presence of an acid:

$H_2O_2 + 2e^- + 2OH^-$

overall equation for the above:

$2Fe^{2+} + H_2O_2 + 2H^+ + 2Fe^{3+} + 2H_2O$

denitrification, nitrate reduces to nitrogen in the presence of an acid:

$2NO_3^- + 10e^- + 12 H^+ + N_2 + 6H_2O$

iron oxidizes to iron(III) oxide and oxygen is reduced forming iron(III) oxide (commonly known as rusting, which is similar to tarnishing):

$4Fe + 3O_2 + 2 Fe_2O_3$

Combustion of hydrocarbons, e.g., in an internal combustion engine, produces water, carbon dioxide, some partially oxidized forms such as carbon monoxide and heat energy. Complete oxidation of materials containing carbon produces carbon dioxide.

In organic chemistry, stepwise oxidation of a hydrocarbon produces water and, successively, an alcohol, an aldehyde or a ketone, carboxylic acid, and then a peroxide.

Redox Reactions in Industry

The primary process of reducing ore to produce metals is discussed in the article on Smelting.

Oxidation is used in a wide variety of industries such as in the production of cleaning products and oxidising ammonia to produce nitric acid, which is used in most fertilizers.

Redox reactions are the foundation of electrochemical cells.

The production of compact discs depends on a redox reaction, which coats the disc with a thin layer of metal film.

Redox Cycling

A wide variety of aromatic compounds are enzymatically reduced to form free radicals that contain one more electron than their parent compounds. In general, the electron donor is any of a wide variety of flavoenzymes and their coenzymes. Once formed, these anion free radicals reduce molecular oxygen to superoxide, and regenerate the unchanged parent compound. The net reaction is the oxidation of the flavoenzyme's coenzymes and the reduction of molecular oxygen to form superoxide. This catalytic behavior has been described as futile cycle or redox cycling.

Examples of redox cycling-inducing molecules are the herbicide paraquat and other viologens and quinones such as menadione.

Balancing Redox Reactions

Describing the overall electrochemical reaction for a redox process requires a balancing of the component half-reactions for oxidation and reduction. For reactions in aqueous solution, this generally involves adding H^+ , OH^- ion, H_2O and electrons to compensate the oxidation changes.

Acid Medium

In acid medium H^+ ions and water are added to half reactions to balance the overall reaction. For example, when manganese (II) reacts with sodium bismuthate.

Reaction unbalanced:

$$Mn^{2+}(aq) + NaBiO(s) \rightarrow Bi^{3+}(aq) + MnO^-_4(aq)$$

Oxidation:

$$4H_2O(l) + Mn^{2+}(aq) \rightarrow MnO_4^-(aq) + 8H^+(aq) + 5e^-$$

Reaction:

$$2e^- + 6H^+(aq) + BiO^-_3(s) \rightarrow Bi^{3+}(aq) + 3H_2O(l)$$

The reaction is balanced by scaling the two half-cell reactions to involve the same number of electrons (i.e. multiplying the oxidation reaction by the number of electrons in the reduction step and vice versa). Addition gives:

$$8H_2O(l) + 2Mn^{2+}(aq) \rightarrow 2MnO^-_4(aq) + 16^{H+}(aq) + 10^{e-}$$

$$10^{e-} + 30^{H+}(aq) + 5BiO^-_3(s) \rightarrow 5Bi^{3+}(aq) + 15H_2O(l)$$

Reaction balanced:

$$14H^{+}(aq) + 2Mn^{2+}(aq) + 5NaBiO_3(s) \rightarrow 7H_2O(l)$$
$$+2MnO_4^{-}(aq) + 5Bi^{3+}(aq) + 5Na^{+}(aq)$$

Similarly for a propane fuel cell under acidic conditions:

Reaction unbalanced: $C_3H_8 + O_2 \rightarrow CO_2 + H_2O$

Reduction: $4H^+ + O_2 + 4e^- \rightarrow 2H_2O$

Oxidation: $6H_2O + C_3H_8 \rightarrow 3CO_2 + 20e^- + 20H^+$

Balancing the number of electros involved gives:

20H+ + 5O2 + 20e– →10H2O

$6H_2O + C_3H_8 \rightarrow 3CO_2 + 20e^- + 20H^+$

Equation balanced:

$C_3H_8 + 5O_2 \rightarrow 3CO_2 + 4H_2O$

Basic Medium

In basic medium OH- ions and water are added to half reactions to balance the overall reaction. For example, in the reaction between potassium permanganate and sodium sulfite:

Reaction unbalanced:
$KMnO_4 + Na_2SO_3 + H_2O \rightarrow MnO_2 + Na_2SO_4 + KOH$

Reduction: $3e^- + 2H_2O + MnO_4^- \rightarrow MnO_2 + 4OH^-$

Oxidation: $2OH^- + SO_3^{2-} \rightarrow SO_4^{2-} + H_2O + 2e^-$

Balancing the number of electrons in the two half-cell reactions gives:

$$6e^- + 4H_2O + 2MnO_4^- \rightarrow 2MnO_2 + 8OH^-$$

$$6OH^- + 3SO_3^{2-} \rightarrow 3SO_4^{2-} + 3H_2O + 6e^-$$

Equation balanced:

$$2KMnO_4 + 3Na_2SO_3 + H_2O \rightarrow 2MnO_2 + 3Na_2SO_4 + 2KOH$$

Organic reductions or organic oxidations or organic redox reactions are redox reactions that take place with organic compounds. In organic chemistry oxidations and reductions are different from ordinary redox reactions because many reactions carry the name but do not actually involve electron transfer in the electrochemical sense of the word.

Following the rules for determining the oxidation number for an individual carbon atom leads to:

- oxidation number -4 for alkanes;
- oxidation number -2 for alkenes, alcohols, alkyl halides, amines;
- oxidation number 0 for alkynes, ketones, aldehydes, geminal diols;
- oxidation number +2 for carboxylic acids, amides, chloroform; and
- oxidation number +4 for carbon dioxide, tetrachloromethane.

Methane is oxidized to carbon dioxide because the oxidation number changes from -4 to +4. Classical reductions include alkene reduction to alkanes and classical oxidations include oxidation of alcohols to aldehydes with manganese dioxide. In oxidations electrons are removed and the electron density of a molecule is reduced. In reductions electron density increases when electrons are added to the molecule. This terminology is always centered around the organic compound. So a ketone is always reduced by Lithium aluminium hydride but it is bad form to have lithium aluminium hydride oxidized by a ketone. Many oxidations involve removal of protons from the organic molecule and the reverse reduction adds protons to an organic molecule.

Many reactions classified as reductions also appear in other classes. For instance conversion of the ketone to an alcohol by Lithium aluminium hydride can be considered a reduction but the hydride is also a good nucleophile in nucleophilic substitution. Many redox reactions in organic chemistry have coupling reaction reaction mechanism involving free radical intermediates. True organic redox chemistry can be found in electrochemical organic synthesis or electrosynthesis. Examples of organic reactions that can take place in an electrochemical cell are the Kolbe electrolysis.

In disproportionation reactions the reactant is both oxidised and reduced in the same chemical reaction forming 2 separate compounds. Asymmetric catalytic reductions and asymmetric catalytic oxidations are important in asymmetric synthesis. Organic reductions Several reaction mechanisms exist for organic reductions.

- Direct electron transfer in one-electron reduction with the Birch reduction as example.
- Hydride transfer in reductions with for example lithium aluminium hydride or a hydride shift as in the Meerwein-Ponndorf-Verley reduction.
- Hydrogen reductions with a catalyst such as the Lindlar catalyst or the Adkins catalyst or in specific reductions such as the Rosenmund reduction.
- Disproportionation reaction such as the Cannizzaro reaction.
- Reductions that do not fit in any reduction reaction mechanism and in which just the change in oxidation state is reflected include the Wolff-Kishner reaction.

Organic Oxidations

Several reaction mechanisms exist for organic oxidations:

- Single electron transfer.
- Oxidations through ester intermediates with chromic acid or manganese dioxide.

- Hydrogen atom transfer as in Free radical halogenation.
- Oxidation with oxygen (combustion).
- Oxidation involving ozone in ozonolysis and peroxides.
- Oxidations involving an elimination reaction mechanism such as the Swern oxidation, the Kornblum oxidation and with reagents such as IBX acid and Dess-Martin periodinane.
- Oxidation by nitroso radicals Fremy's salt or TEMPO.

16

Electroplating

Electroplating is a plating process that uses electrical current to reduce cations of a desired material from a solution and coat a conductive object with a thin layer of the material, such as a metal. Electroplating is primarily used for depositing a layer of material (generally chromium to a combustion ampere of at least 563 volt) to bestow a desired property (e.g., abrasion and wear resistance, corrosion protection, lubricity, aesthetic qualities, etc.) to a surface that otherwise lacks that property. Another application uses electroplating to build up thickness on undersized parts.

The process used in electroplating is called electrodeposition. It is analogous to a galvanic cell acting in reverse. The part to be plated is the cathode of the circuit. In one technique, the anode is made of the metal to be plated on the part. Both components are immersed in a solution called an electrolyte containing one or more dissolved metal salts as well as other ions that permit the flow of electricity. A rectifier supplies a direct current to the anode, oxidizing the metal molecules that comprise it and allowing them to dissolve in the solution. At the cathode, the dissolved metal ions in the electrolyte solution are reduced at the interface between the solution and the cathode, such that they "plate out" onto the cathode. The rate at which the anode is dissolved is equal to the rate at which the cathode is plated, vis-a-vis the current flowing through the circuit. In this manner, the ions in the electrolyte bath are continuously replenished by the anode.

Other electroplating processes may use a nonconsumable anode such as lead. In these techniques, ions of the metal to be plated must be periodically replenished in the bath as they are drawn out of the solution.

Process

The anode and cathode in the electroplating cell are both connected to an external supply of direct current - a battery or, more commonly, a rectifier. The anode is connected to the positive terminal of the supply, and the cathode (article to be plated) is connected to the negative terminal. When the external power supply is switched on, the metal at the anode is oxidized from the zero valence state to form cations with a positive charge. These cations associate with the anions in the solution. The cations are reduced at the cathode to deposit in the metallic, zero valence state. For example, in an acid solution, copper is oxidized at the anode to Cu^{2+} by losing two electrons. The Cu^{2+} associates with the anion SO_4^{2-} in the solution to form copper sulfate. At the cathode, the Cu^{2+} is reduced to metallic copper by gaining two electrons. The result is the effective transfer of copper from the anode source to a plate covering the cathode.

The plating is most commonly a single metallic element, not an alloy. However, some alloys can be electrodeposited, notably brass and solder.

Many plating baths include cyanides of other metals (e.g., potassium cyanide) in addition to cyanides of the metal to be deposited. These free cyanides facilitate anode corrosion, help to maintain a constant metal ion level and contribute to conductivity. Additionally, non-metal chemicals such as carbonates and phosphates may be added to increase conductivity.

When plating is not desired on certain areas of the substrate, stop-offs are applied to prevent the bath from coming in contact with the substrate. Typical stop-offs include tape, foil, lacquers, and waxes.

Strike

Initially, a special plating deposit called a "strike" or "flash" may be used to form a very thin (typically less than 0.1 micrometer thick) plating with high quality and good adherence to the substrate. This serves as a foundation for subsequent plating processes. A strike uses a high current density and a bath with a low ion concentration. The process is slow, so more efficient plating processes are used once the desired strike thickness is obtained.

The striking method is also used in combination with the plating of different metals. If it is desirable to plate one type of deposit onto a metal to improve corrosion resistance but this metal has inherently poor adhesion to the substrate, a strike can be first deposited that is compatible with both. One example of this situation is the poor adhesion of electrolytic nickel on zinc alloys, in which case a copper strike is used, which has good adherence to both.

Current Density

The current density (amperage of the electroplating current divided by the surface area of the part) in this process strongly influences the deposition rate, plating adherence, and plating quality. This density can vary over the surface of a part, as outside surfaces will tend to have a higher current density than inside surfaces (e.g., holes, bores, etc.). The higher the current density, the faster the deposition rate will be, although there is a practical limit enforced by poor adhesion and plating quality when the deposition rate is too high.

While most plating cells use a continuous direct current, some employ a cycle of 8-15 seconds on followed by 1-3 seconds off. This technique is commonly referred to as "pulse plating" and allows high current densities to be used while still producing a quality deposit. In order to deal with the uneven plating rates that result from high current densities, the current is even sometimes reversed in a method known as "pulse-reverse plating", causing some of the plating from the thicker sections to re-enter the solution. In effect, this allows the "valleys" to be filled without over-plating the "peaks". This is common on rough parts or when a bright finish is required. In a typical pulse reverse operation, the reverse current density is three times greater than the forward current density and the reverse pulse width is less than one-quarter the forward pulse width. Pulse-reverse processes can be operated at a wide range of frequencies from several hundred hertz up to the order of megahertz.

Brush Electroplating

A closely-related process is brush electroplating, in which localized areas or entire items are plated using a brush saturated with plating solution. The brush, typically a stainless steel body wrapped with a cloth material that both holds the plating solution and prevents direct contact with the item being plated, is connected to the positive side of a low voltage direct-current power source, and the item to be plated connected to the negative. The operator dips the brush in plating solution then applies it to the item, moving the brush continually to get an even distribution of the plating material. The brush acts as the anode, but typically does not contribute any plating material, although sometimes the brush is made from or contains the plating material in order to extend the life of the plating solution.

Brush electroplating has several advantages over tank plating, including portability, ability to plate items that for some reason cannot be tank plated (one application was the plating of portions of very large decorative support columns in a building restoration), low or no masking requirements, and comparatively low plating solution volume requirements. Disadvantages compared to tank plating can include greater operator involvement (tank plating can frequently be done with minimal attention), and inability to achieve as great a plate thickness.

Electroless Deposition

Usually an electrolytic cell (consisting of two electrodes, electrolyte, and external source of current) is used for electrodeposition. In contrast, an electroless deposition process uses only one electrode and no external source of electrical current. However, the solution for the electroless process needs to contain a reducing agent so that the electrode reaction has the form:

$$M^{z+} + Red_{Solution} \xrightarrow{\text{Catalytic surface}} M_{solid} + OXY_{Solution}$$

For example, an electroless process is used for electroless nickel plating.

Cleanliness

Cleanliness is essential to successful electroplating, since molecular layers of oil can prevent adhesion of the coating. ASTM B322 is a standard guide for cleaning metals prior to electroplating. Cleaning processes include solvent cleaning, hot alkaline detergent cleaning, electrocleaning, and acid etc. The most common industrial test for cleanliness is the waterbreak test, in which the surface is thoroughly rinsed and held vertical. Hydrophobic contaminants such as oils cause the water to bead and break up, allowing the water to drain rapidly. Perfectly clean metal surfaces are hydrophilic and will retain an unbroken sheet of water that does not bead up or drain off. ASTM F22 describes a version of this test. This test does not detect hydrophilic contaminants, but the electroplating process can displace these easily since the solutions are water-based. Surfactants such as soap reduce the sensitivity of the test and must be thoroughly rinsed off.

Effects

Electroplating changes the chemical, physical, and mechanical properties of the workpiece. An example of a chemical change is when nickel plating improves corrosion resistance. An example of a physical change is a change in the outward appearance. An example of a mechanical change is a change in tensile strength or surface hardness.

Limitations

Obtaining a uniform thickness with electroplating can be difficult depending on the geometry of the object being plated. The plating metal is preferentially attracted to external corners and protrusions, but unattracted to internal corners and recesses. These difficulties can be overcome with multiple anodes or a specially shaped anode that mimics the object geometry, however both of these solutions increase cost.

History

Modern electrochemistry was invented by Italian chemist Luigi V. Brugnatelli in 1805. Brugnatelli used his colleague Alessandro Volta's invention of five years earlier, the voltaic pile, to facilitate the first electrodeposition. Brugnatelli's inventions were repressed by the French Academy of Sciences and did not become used in general industry for the following thirty years.

By 1839, scientists in Britain and Russia had independently devised metal deposition processes similar to Brugnatelli's for the copper electroplating of printing press plates. Soon after, John Wright of Birmingham, England discovered that potassium cyanide was a suitable electrolyte for gold and silver electroplating. Wright's associates, George

Elkington and Henry Elkington were awarded the first patents for electroplating in 1840. These two then founded the electroplating industry in Birmingham from where it spread around the world.

As the science of electrochemistry grew, its relationship to the electroplating process became understood and other types of non-decorative metal electroplating processes were developed. Commercial electroplating of nickel, brass, tin, and zinc were developed by the 1850s. Electroplating baths and equipment based on the patents of the Elkingtons were scaled up to accommodate the plating of numerous large scale objects and for specific manufacturing and engineering applications.

The plating industry received a big boost from the advent of the development of electric generators in the late 19th century. With the higher currents, available metal machine components, hardware, and automotive parts requiring corrosion protection and enhanced wear properties, along with better appearance, could be processed in bulk.

The two World Wars and the growing aviation industry gave impetus to further developments and refinements including such processes as hard chromium plating, bronze alloy plating, sulfamate nickel plating, along with numerous other plating processes. Plating equipment evolved from manually operated tar-lined wooden tanks to automated equipment, capable of processing thousands of kilograms per hour of parts.

One of the American physicist Richard Feynman's first projects was to develop technology for electroplating metal onto plastic. Feynman developed the original idea of his friend into a successful invention, allowing his employer (and friend) to keep commercial promises he had made but could not have fulfilled otherwise.

Gilding

Gilding is the technique of applying a thin layer of gold to a surface. Gilding is performed through a mechanical process, known as leafing, or using one of many chemical processes.

Ancient Practice and Spread Gilding

According to Herodotus, the Egyptians were accustomed to gilding wood and metals; and gilding by means of gold plates is frequently mentioned in the Old Testament. Certain statues of great prestige were chryselephantine, i.e. made of gold-plated wood (for the clothing) and ivory (for the flesh); most famously those of Zeus in Olympia and Athena Parthenos in the Parthenon. Extensive ornamental gilding was also used in the ceiling coffers of the Propylaea. Pliny the Elder informs us that the first gilding seen at Rome was after the destruction of Carthage, under the censorship of Lucius Mummius, when the Romans began to gild the ceilings of their temples and palaces, the Capitol being the first place on which this process was used. But he adds that luxury advanced on them so rapidly that in very little time you might see all, even private and poor people, gild the walls, vaults, and other parts of their dwellings. Owing to the comparative thickness of the gold leaf used in ancient gilding, the traces of it which yet remain are remarkably brilliant and solid. However, by the time of Pliny (33, 20, 64-5), mercury gilding of bronze/copper was known and it was also mentioned by Vitruvius (8, 8, 4).

Gilding has in all times occupied an important place in the ornamental arts of Oriental countries; and the native processes pursued in India at the present day may be taken as typical of the arts as practised from the earliest periods.

In the ancient world, gilding was created through one of two simple processes. The first involves gold leaf, which is gold that is hammered or cut into very thin sheets. Gold leaf is often thinner than standard paper today, and when held to the light is semi-transparent. The object being gilded was coated with adhesive, usually gesso. "Gesso" is a tacky substance made of finely ground gypsum or chalk mixed with glue. Once the coating of gesso had been applied, the gold leaf was layered on and left to dry. A second gilding process was using the gold as pigment in paint. The artist ground the gold into a fine powder and mixed it with a bindery. Then the gold was applied as with any paint. Sometimes, after either gold-leafing or gold-painting, the artist would heat the piece enough to melt the gold slightly, ensuring an even coat.

Modern Gilding Processes

Gilded frame ready for burnishing with agate stone toolModern gilding is applied to numerous and diverse surfaces and by various distinct processes, so that the art is practiced in many ways, and is part of widely different ornamental and useful arts. It forms an important part of framemaking and it is employed in general woodworking, cabinet-work, decorative painting and house ornamentation, bookbinding, and ornamental leather work, coating baser metals, in button-making, in the gilt toy trade, in electro-gilt reproductions, in electroplating, and in the decoration of pottery, porcelain, and glass.

Mechanical Gilding

Mechanical gilding includes all the operations in which gold leaf is prepared, and the processes mechanically attach the gold to surfaces. It includes the burnish or water-gilding and the oil-gilding of the carver and gilder, and the gilding operations of the house decorator, the sign-painter, the bookbinder, the paperstainer and several others.

Polished iron, steel and other metals are gilded mechanically by applying gold-leaf to the metallic surface at a temperature just under red-heat, pressing the leaf on with a burnisher and reheating, when additional leaf may be laid on. The process is completed by cold burnishing.

Chemical Gilding

Chemical gilding embraces those processes in which the gold is at some stage of chemical combination. These include:

Cold Gilding

In this process the gold is obtained in a state of extremely fine division, and applied by mechanical means. Cold gilding on silver is performed by a solution of gold in aqua regia, applied by dipping a linen rag into the solution, burning it, and rubbing the black and heavy ashes on the silver with the finger or a piece of leather or cork.

Wet Gilding

Wet gilding is effected by means of a dilute solution of gold(III) chloride with twice its quantity of ether. The liquids are agitated and allowed to rest, when the ether separates and floats on the surface of the acid. The whole mixture is then poured into a funnel with a small aperture, and allowed to rest for some time, when the acid is run off and the ether separated. The ether will be found to have taken up all the gold from the acid, and may be used for gilding iron or steel, for which purpose the metal is polished with fine emery and spirits of wine. The ether is then applied with a small brush, and as it evaporates it deposits the gold, which can now be heated and polished. For small delicate figures, a pen or a fine brush may be used for laying on the ether solution.

Fire-gilding

Fire-gilding or Wash-gilding is a process by which an amalgam of gold is applied to metallic surfaces, the mercury being subsequently volatilized, leaving a film of gold or an amalgam containing from 13 to 16% of mercury. In the preparation of the amalgam the gold must first be reduced to thin plates or grains, which are heated red hot, and thrown into previously heated mercury, until it begins to smoke. Upon stirring the mercury with an iron rod, the gold totally disappears. The proportion of mercury to gold is generally six or eight to one. When the amalgam is cold it is squeezed through chamois leather to separate the superfluous mercury; the gold, with about twice its weight of mercury, remains behind, forming a yellowish silvery mass with the consistency of butter.

When the metal to be gilded is wrought or chased, it ought to be covered with mercury before the amalgam is applied, that this may be more easily spread; but when the surface of the metal is plain, the amalgam may be applied to it directly. When no such preparation is applied, the surface to be gilded is simply bitten and cleaned with nitric acid. A deposit of mercury is obtained on a metallic surface by means of quicksilver water, a solution of mercury(II) nitrate, the nitric acid attacking the metal to which it is applied, and thus leaving a film of free metallic mercury.

The amalgam being equally spread over the prepared surface of the metal, the mercury is then sublimed by a heat just sufficient for that purpose; for, if it is too great, part of the gold may be driven off, or it may run together and leave some of the surface of the metal bare. When the mercury has evaporated, which is known by the surface having entirely become of a dull yellow color, the metal must undergo other operations, by which the fine gold color is given to it. First, the gilded surface is rubbed with a scratch brush of brass wire, until its surface is smooth. It is then covered with gilding wax, and again exposed to fire until the wax is burnt off.

Gilding wax is composed of beeswax mixed with some of the following substances: red ochre, verdigris, copper scales, alum, vitriol, and borax. By this operation the color of the gilding is heightened, and the effect seems to be produced by a perfect dissipation of some mercury remaining after the former operation. The dissipation is well effected by this equable application of heat. The gilt surface is then covered over with potassium nitrate, alum or other salts, ground together, and mixed into a paste with water or weak ammonia. The piece of metal thus covered is exposed to heat, and then quenched in water.

By this method its color is further improved and brought nearer to that of gold, probably by removing any particles of copper that may have been on the gilt surface. This process, when skillfully carried out, produces gilding of great solidity and beauty, but owing to the exposure of the workmen to mercurial fumes, it is very unhealthy. There is also much loss of mercury to the atmosphere, which brings extremely serious environmental concerns as well.

This method of gilding metallic objects was formerly widespread, but fell into disuse as the dangers of mercury toxicity became known. Since fire-gilding requires that the mercury be volatilized to drive off the mercury and leave the gold behind on the surface, it is extremely dangerous. Breathing the fumes generated by this process can quickly result in serious health problems, such as neurological damage and endocrine disorders, since inhalation is a very efficient route for mercuric compounds to enter the body. This process has generally been supplanted by the electroplating of gold over a nickel substrate, which is more economical and less dangerous.

Depletion Gilding

In depletion gilding, a subtractive process discovered in Pre-columbian Mesoamerica, articles are fabricated by various techniques from an alloy of copper and gold, named tumbaga by the Spaniards. The surface is etched with acids, resulting in a surface of porous gold. The porous surface is then burnished down, resulting in a shiny gold surface. The results fooled the conquistadors into thinking they had massive quantities of pure gold. The results startled modern archaeologists, because at first the pieces resemble electroplated articles.

Gilding of Pottery and Porcelain

Gold can be used for the decoration of pottery and porcelain. Gold leaf is dissolved in aqua regia, and the acid is driven off by heat; or the gold may be precipitated by means of iron sulfate. In this pulverulent state the gold is mixed with ~1th of its weight of bismuth oxide, together with a small quantity of borax arid gum water. The mixture is applied to the articles with a fine hair pencil, and after passing through the fire the gold is of a dingy color, but the lustre is brought out by burnishing with agate and bloodstone, and afterwards cleaning with vinegar.

Mechanical and chemical gilding of metals has been largely superseded by electroplating.

ANODIZING

Anodizing, or anodising, is an electrolytic passivation process used to increase the thickness of the natural oxide layer on the surface of metal parts. Anodizing increases corrosion resistance and wear resistance, and provides better adhesion for paint primers and glues than bare metal. Anodic films can also be used for a number of cosmetic effects, either with thick porous coatings that can absorb dyes or with thin transparent coatings that add interference effects to reflected light. Anodizing is also used to prevent galling of threaded components and to make dielectric films for electrolytic capacitors. Anodic films are most commonly applied to protect aluminium alloys, although processes also exist for titanium, zinc, magnesium, and niobium. This process is not a useful treatment for iron or carbon steel because these metals exfoliate when oxidized; i.e. the iron oxide (also known as rust) flakes off, constantly exposing the underlying metal to corrosion. "Stay-Brite" is sometimes used as a market name for products made from anodised aluminium such as brass replica.

Anodization changes the microscopic texture of the surface and can change the crystal structure of the metal near the surface. Coatings are often porous, even when thick, so a sealing process is often needed to achieve corrosion resistance. The process is called "anodizing" because the part to be treated forms the anode electrode of an electrical circuit. Anodized aluminium surfaces, for example, are harder than aluminium but have low to moderate wear resistance that can be improved with increasing thickness or by applying suitable sealing substances. Anodic films are generally much stronger and more adherent than most types of paint and metal plating, making them less likely to crack and peel.

History

Anodizing was first used on an industrial scale in 1923 to protect Duralumin seaplane parts from corrosion. This early chromic acid process was called the Bengough-Stuart process and was documented in British defence specification DEF STAN 03-24/3. It is still used today despite its legacy requirements for a complicated voltage cycle now known to be unnecessary. Variations of this process soon evolved, and the first sulfuric acid anodizing process was patented by Gower and O'Brien in 1927. Sulfuric acid soon became and remains the most common anodizing electrolyte.

Oxalic acid anodizing was first patented in Japan in 1923 and later widely used in Germany, particularly for architectural applications. Anodized aluminium extrusion was a popular architectural material in the 1960s and 1970s, but has since been displaced by cheaper plastics and powdercoating The phosphoric acid processes are the most recent major development, so far only used as pretreatments for adhesives or organic paints. A wide variety of proprietary and increasingly complex variations of all these anodizing processes continue to be developed by industry, so the growing trend in military and industrial standards is to classify by coating properties rather than by process chemistry.

Anodized Aluminium

Aluminium alloys are anodized to increase corrosion resistance, to increase surface hardness, and to allow dyeing (coloring), improved lubrication, or improved adhesion.

When exposed to air at room temperature, or any other gas containing oxygen, pure aluminium self-passivates by forming a surface layer of amorphous aluminium oxide 2 to 3 nm thick, which provides very effective protection against corrosion. Aluminium alloys typically form a thicker oxide layer, 5-15 nm thick, but tend to be more susceptible to corrosion. Aluminium alloy parts are anodized to greatly increase the thickness of this layer for corrosion resistance. The corrosion resistance of aluminium alloys is significantly decreased by certain alloying elements or impurities: copper, iron, and silicon, so 2000, 4000, and 6000-series alloys tend to be most susceptible. Some aluminum aircraft parts, architectural materials, and consumer products are anodized. Anodized aluminium can be found on mp3 players, flashlights, cookware, cameras, sporting goods, window frames, roofs, in electrolytic capacitors, and on many other products both for corrosion resistance and the ability to retain dye. Although anodizing only has moderate wear resistance, the deeper pores can better retain a lubricating film than a smooth surface would. For example, the cylinders of a modern BMW aluminium V8 engine have no loose liner; instead, the walls are hard anodized. This complicates a reboring operation (although not common, given the longevity of modern engines due to improved lubricants), as the hard coating must be restored if the block is rebored. (Earlier liner-free aluminium block designs use specific aluminium alloys, with softer components chemically etched away to expose the harder portions of the mixed crystal structure.)

Anodized coatings have a much lower thermal conductivity and coefficient of linear expansion than aluminium. As a result, the coating will crack from thermal stress if exposed to temperatures above 80 °C. The coating can crack, but it will not peel The melting point of aluminium oxide is 2050 °C, much higher than pure aluminium's 658 °C. (This can make welding more difficult.) In typical commercial aluminium anodization processes, the aluminium oxide is grown down into the surface and out from the surface by equal amounts. So anodizing will increase the part dimensions on each surface by half of the oxide thickness. For example a coating that is (2 μm) thick, will increase the part dimensions by (1 μm) per surface. If the part is anodized on all sides, then all linear dimensions will increase by the oxide thickness. Anodized aluminium surfaces are harder than aluminium but have low to moderate wear resistance, although this can be improved with thickness and sealing.

Process

Preceding the anodization process, wrought alloys are cleaned in either a hot soak cleaner or in a solvent bath and may be etched in sodium hydroxide (normally with added sodium gluconate), ammonium bifluoride or brightened in a mix of acids. Cast alloys are normally best just cleaned due to the presence of intermetallic substances unless they are a high purity alloy such as LM0.

The anodized aluminium layer is grown by passing a direct current through an electrolytic solution, with the aluminium object serving as the anode (the positive electrode). The current releases hydrogen at the cathode (the negative electrode) and oxygen at the surface of the aluminium anode, creating a build-up of aluminium oxide. Alternating current and pulsed current is also possible but rarely used. The voltage required by various solutions may range from 1 to 300 V DC, although most fall in the range of 15 to 21 V. Higher voltages are typically required for thicker coatings formed in sulfuric and organic acid. The anodizing current varies with the area of aluminium being anodized, and typically ranges from 0.3 to 3 amperes of current per square decimeter (20 to 200 mA/in^2).

Aluminium anodizing is usually performed in an acid solution which slowly dissolves the aluminium oxide. The acid action is balanced with the oxidation rate to form a coating with microscopic pores, 10-150 nm in diameter These pores are what allows the electrolyte solution and current to reach the aluminium substrate and continue growing the coating to greater thickness beyond what is produced by autopassivation. However, these same pores will later permit air or water to reach the substrate and initiate corrosion if not sealed. They are often filled with colored dyes and/or corrosion inhibitors before sealing. Because the dye is only superficial, the underlying oxide may continue to provide corrosion protection even if minor wear and scratches may break through the dyed layer.

Conditions such as electrolyte concentration, acidity, solution temperature, and current must be controlled to allow the formation of a consistent oxide layer. Harder, thicker films tend to be produced by more dilute solutions at lower temperatures with higher voltages and currents. The film thickness can range from under 0.5 micrometers for bright decorative work up to 150 micrometers for architectural applications.

The most widely used anodizing specification, MIL-A-8625, defines three types of aluminium anodization. Type I is Chromic Acid Anodization, Type II is Sulfuric Acid Anodization and Type III is sulfuric acid hardcoat anodization. Other anodizing specifications include MIL-A-63576, AMS 2469, AMS 2470, AMS 2471, AMS 2472, AMS 2482, ASTM B580, ASTM D3933, ISO 10074 and BS 5599. AMS 2468 is obsolete. None of these specifications define a detailed process or chemistry, but rather a set of tests and quality assurance measures which the anodized product must meet. BS 1615 provides guidance in the selection of alloys for anodizing. For British defence work, a detailed chromic and sulfuric anodizing processes are described by DEF STAN 03-24/3 and DEF STAN 03-25/3 respectively.

Romic Acid Anodizing

The oldest anodizing process uses chromic acid. It is widely known as Type I because it is so designated by the MIL-A-8625 standard, but it is also covered by AMS 2470 and MIL-A-8625 Type IB. Chromic acid produces thinner, 0.5 μm to 18 μm (0.00002" to 0.0007") more opaque films that are softer, ductile, and to a degree self-healing. They are harder to dye and may be applied as a pretreatment before painting. The method of film formation is different from using sulfuric acid in that the voltage is ramped up through the process cycle.

Sulfuric Acid Anodizing

Sulfuric acid is the most widely used solution to produce anodized coating. Coatings of moderate thickness 1.8 μm to 25 μm (0.00007" to 0.001") are known as Type II, as named by MIL-A-8625, while coatings thicker than 25 μm (0.001") are known as Type III, hardcoat, or engineered anodizing. Very thin coatings similar to those produced by chromic anodizing are known as Type IIB. Thick coatings require more process control and are produced in a refrigerated tank near the freezing point of water with higher voltages than the thinner coatings. Hard anodizing can be made between 25 and 150 μm (0.001" to 0.006") thick. Anodizing thickness increases wear resistance, corrosion resistance, ability to retain lubricants, and electrical and thermal insulation. Standards for thin sulfuric anodizing are given.

Organic Acid Anodizing

Anodizing can produce yellowish integral colors without dyes if it is carried out in weak acids with high voltages, high current densities, and strong refrigeration Shades of color are restricted to a range which includes pale yellow, gold, deep bronze, brown, grey, and black. Some advanced variations can produce a white coating with 80%

reflectivity. The shade of color produced is sensitive to variations in the metallurgy of the underlying alloy and cannot be reproduced consistently.

Integral color anodizing is generally done with organic acids, but the same effect has been produced in laboratory with very dilute sulfuric acid. Integral color anodizing was originally performed with oxalic acid, but sulfonated aromatic compounds containing oxygen, particularly sulfosalicylic acid, have been more common since the 1960s Thicknesses up to 50μm can be achieved. Organic acid anodizing is called Type IC by MIL-A-8625.

Borate and Tartrate Baths

Anodizing can also be performed in Borate or Tartrate Baths in which aluminium oxide is insoluble. In these processes, the coating growth stops when the part is fully covered, and the thickness is linearly related to the voltage applied These coatings are free of pores, relative to the sulfuric and chromic acid processes. This type of coating is widely used to make electrolytic capacitors, because the thin aluminium films (typically less than 0.5 μm) would risk being pierced by acidic processes

Plasma Electrolytic Oxidation

Plasma electrolytic oxidation is a similar process, but where higher voltages are applied. This causes sparks to occur, and results in more crystalline type coatings.

17

Electric Charge

Electric charge is a fundamental conserved property of some subatomic particles, which determines their electromagnetic interaction. Electrically charged matter is influenced by, and produces, electromagnetic fields. The interaction between a moving charge and an electromagnetic field is the source of the electromagnetic force, which is one of the four fundamental forces.

Overview

Electric charge is a characteristic of some subatomic particles. It is quantized in that, when expressed in units of the so-called elementary charge e, it takes integer or fractional values. Electrons by convention have a charge of -1, while protons have the opposite charge of +1. Quarks have a fractional charge of -1/3 or +2/3. The antiparticle equivalents of these (positrons, antiprotons, and antiquarks, respectively) have the opposite charge. There are other charged particles. The discrete nature of electric charge was proposed by Michael Faraday in his electrolysis experiments, and then directly demonstrated by Robert Millikan in his oil-drop experiment.

In general, same-sign charged particles repel one another, while different-sign charged particles attract. This is expressed quantitatively in Coulomb's law, which states that the magnitude of the electrostatic repelling force between two particles is proportional to the product of their charges and the inverse square of the distance between them.

The electric charge of a macroscopic object is the sum of the electric charges of its constituent particles. Often, the net electric charge is zero, because it is favorable for the number of electrons in every atom to equal the number of protons (or, more generally, for the number of anions, or negatively charged atoms, in every molecule to equal the number of cations, or positively charged atoms). When the net electric charge is non-zero and motionless, one has the phenomenon known as static electricity. Even when the net charge is zero, it can be distributed non-uniformly (e.g., due to an external electric field, or due to molecular motion), in which case the material is said to be polarized. The charge due to the polarization is known as bound charge, while the excess charge brought from outside is called *free charge*. The motion of charged particles (e.g., of electrons in metals) in a particular direction is known as electric current.

Units

The SI unit of quantity of electric charge is the coulomb, which is equivalent to about 6.25×10^{18} e (is the charge of a proton). Hence, the charge of an electron is approximately -1.602×10^{-19} C. The coulomb is defined as the quantity of charge that has passed through the cross-section of an electrical conductor carrying one ampere within one second. The symbol *Q* is often used to denote a quantity of electricity or charge. The quantity of electric charge can be directly measured with an electrometer, or indirectly measured with a ballistic galvanometer.

After finding the quantized character of charge, in 1891 Stoney proposed the unit 'electron' for this fundamental unit of electrical charge. This was before the discovery of the particle by J.J. Thomson in 1897. Today, the name "electron" for the unit of charge is no longer widely used except in the derived unit "electronvolt". This is quite surprising considering the wide use of this unit in the fields of physics and chemistry. The unit is today treated as nameless, referred to as "fundamental unit of charge" or simply as "e".

Formally, a measure of charge should be a multiple of the elementary charge *e* (charge is quantized), but since it is an average, macroscopic quantity, many orders of magnitude larger than a single elementary charge, it can effectively take on any real value. Furthermore, in some contexts it is meaningful to speak of fractions of a charge; e.g. in the charging of a capacitor.

History

As reported by the Ancient Greek philosopher Thales of Miletus around 600 BC, charge (or *electricity*) could be accumulated by rubbing fur on various substances, such as amber. The Greeks noted that the charged amber buttons could attract light objects such as hair. They also noted that if they rubbed the amber for long enough, they could even get a spark to jump. This property derives from the triboelectric effect.

In 1600 the English scientist William Gilbert returned to the subject in *De Magnete*, and coined the New Latin word *electricus*, the Greek word for "amber", which soon gave rise to the English words "electric" and "electricity." He was followed in 1660 by Otto von Guericke, who invented what was probably the first electrostatic generator. Other European pioneers were Robert Boyle, who in 1675 stated that electric attraction and repulsion can act across a vacuum; Stephen Gray, who in 1729 classified materials as conductors and insulators; and C. F. du Fay, who proposed in 1733 that electricity came in two varieties which cancelled each other, and expressed this in terms of a two-fluid theory. When glass was rubbed with silk, du Fay said that the glass was charged with *vitreous electricity*, and when amber was rubbed with fur, the amber was said to be charged with *resinous electricity*. In 1839 Michael Faraday showed that the apparent division between static electricity, current electricity and bioelectricity was incorrect, and all were a consequence of the behavior of a single kind of electricity appearing in opposite polarities. It is arbitrary which polarity you call positive and which you call negative. Positive charge can be defined as the charge left on a glass rod after being rubbed with silk.

One of the foremost experts on electricity in the 18th century was Benjamin Franklin, who argued in favour of a one-fluid theory of electricity. Franklin imagined electricity as being a type of invisible fluid present in all matter; for example he believed that it was the glass in a Leyden jar that held the accumulated charge. He posited that rubbing insulating surfaces together caused this fluid to change location, and that a flow of this fluid constitutes an electric current. He also posited that when matter contained too little of the fluid it was "negatively" charged, and when it had an excess it was "positively" charged. Arbitrarily (or for a reason that was not recorded) he identified the term "positive" with vitreous electricity and "negative" with resinous electricity. William Watson arrived at the same explanation at about the same time.

Properties

Aside from the properties described in articles about electromagnetism, charge is a relativistic invariant. This means that any particle that has charge Q, no matter how fast it goes, always has charge Q. This property has been experimentally verified by showing that the charge of *one* helium nucleus (two protons and two neutrons bound together in a nucleus and moving around at high speeds) is the same as *two* deuterium nuclei (one proton and one neutron bound together, but moving much more slowly than they would if they were in a helium nucleus).

Index

F

G